Teaching Global Awareness with Simulations and Games

Grades 6-12

Steven L. Lamy, et al.

CENTER FOR TEACHING
INTERNATIONAL
RELATIONS

For further information about the other CTIR publications and programs, please call 303-871-3106, or visit our web site at **www.du.edu/ctir.**

CTIR Publications

BRINGING THE WORLD TO YOUR CLASSROOM

CENTER FOR TEACHING
INTERNATIONAL
R E L A T I O N S

University of Denver
Graduate School of International Studies

For over 35 years, the Center for Teaching International Relations (CTIR) has published high quality materials on international studies for use in K–12 classrooms. As an integral part of the University of Denver Graduate School of International Studies, CTIR is dedicated to improving public understanding of international affairs.

CTIR materials are designed to provide a balanced presentation of information with the goal of fostering critical thinking about international issues. Our age-appropriate lesson plans are written in conjunction with award-winning classroom teachers and are strategically presented in a modular format from which teachers can choose the most relevant lessons for their specific classrooms. Each lesson is:

- Activity oriented
- Based on national education content standards
- Designed to help students prepare for standardized testing
- Written to incorporate language arts and logical thinking skills

CTIR materials fit easily into a classroom curriculum because they are based on core subject matters such as economics, history, civics, geography, and science. By addressing these subjects in an international context, students gain both an understanding of contemporary international events as well as the foundations upon which they are based. CTIR materials provide students with tools to successfully navigate an increasingly global environment.

CENTER FOR TEACHING
INTERNATIONAL
R E L A T I O N S

We want to hear from you!

Your comments on this publication will help us develop
materials that suit your needs.

Visit our web site to:

- Complete our survey
- Download *free* materials
- Join our mailing list

www.du.edu/ctir

800-967-2847

Internet Resources

By purchasing this book you now have access to a new service provided by CTIR. The Lesson Hand-Outs and Activities included in this book are now available in an easy to download format on our website. Instead of making copies from the book, we invite you to download all of the handouts at once.

It's quick and easy to do. Just go to **www.du.edu/ctir**, click on Publications, and select Teacher Resources. After filling in your name you will be directed to a list of all CTIR books from which you may choose from any of the titles that you have purchased from us. From here you will need a password to open the file.

The password for *Teaching About Global Awareness with Simulations and Games* is: **Zabros**

(Note: Passwords are case sensitive)

TABLE OF CONTENTS

Teaching Global Awareness with Simulations and Games allows students to participate in realistic global situations involving people from all walks of life: politicians, diplomats, farmers, sharecroppers, consumers, United Nations officials, and international business executives. Activities in this unit give students the chance to experience and understand international/intercultural situations through participation.

Three of the simulations included in this unit are "Coping," "Self-Defense: A Simulation of World War I," and "Going After Mr. Goodbar." "Coping" presents a situation that has students become member of ethnic groups trying to retain their ethnic identity but also live peacefully in a very diverse ethnic community. "Self-Defense: A Simulations of World War I" has students divide into countries with pseudonyms such as Northland, Southland, and Grainland; and unknowingly replay the actions leading to World War I. "Going After Mr. Goodbar" has students role play business people whose job is to "build" a candy bar. They not only grasp the concept of interdependence, but also some of its economic ramifications for the world's traders.

Topics

Teaching Global Awareness with Simulations and Games covers four global themes of development and technology, world trade and interdependency, politics, and human rights. The simulations and games included in this unit are arranged according to difficulty with sections. For instance, "A Simple but Complex Chocolate Bar" provides an easy simulation for demonstrating the international interdependence needed to make a chocolate bar. It is followed by a more complex simulation called "World Trade" which builds on the concept skills students learned in the previous activity.

Teaching Strategies

A good simulation simplifies complex situations to make them understandable to participants, but does not sacrifice the integrity of the subject matter. *Teaching Global Awareness with Simulations and Games* tries to provide teachers with simulations that are of that genre. In addition, such simulations give teachers an alternative approach for helping students understand various concepts and content areas.

When and Where to Use the Activities

These activities are designed to be used with students in grades 6-12. Some may be adapted for college classroom use as well. Each activity is labeled with an appropriate grade level. However, most can be revised for use with older or younger students. They are appropriate supplementary materials for courses in social studies, world affairs, political science, business, and geography.

I. DEVELOPMENT AND TECHNOLOGY

Introduction

A primary concern in the study of global affairs is to increase understanding of the acquisition patterns of goods and resources throughout the world. Maldistribution underlies many of the world's most pressing long-term problems, but can goods and resources be divided equitably? In the scramble for pennies, students gain deeper insights into this fundamental global problem.

Objectives

Students will be able to:

• Better understand the acquisition and distribution of world goods, services, and resources.
• Compare and contrast their own views about distribution with the views of others.
• Draw conclusions about the necessity and feasibility of redistributing Earth's resources.

Grade   Level

6-12

Time

One class period

Materials

100 pennies
Paper
Markers, pens, or chalk

Procedure

1. Explain to students that in this game they will have a chance to acquire a great deal of wealth, in fact, 100 percent of the wealth (goods, services, power, resources, etc.) that the world has to offer. Explain that the wealth will be represented by 100 pennies. Tell students there is only one rule they must follow in their acquisition of wealth--they may not at any time touch any member of the class for the rest of the class period.

2. Arrange the room so students won't bump into furniture. Scatter the pennies on the floor. Have students scramble for the pennies, then return to their desks.

3. Ask students to count their pennies. Record the results on the chalkboard. Mark each student's initials next to the number of pennies acquired.

4. Tell students they may, if they wish, give pennies to less wealthy class members. Allow two or three minutes for this exchange.

5. Tell students they will be rewarded according to their wealth. For example: all students who have five or more pennies will receive five extra credit points or they may leave class five minutes early. Develop rewards that suit your particular class situation. They should

be tempting enough to please the "wealthy" and discourage the "poor" and motivate students in their subsequent attempts to either maintain the status quo or redistribute the pennies. At the same time, the rewards should not be threatening enough to alarm students about their progress in class.

6. Tell all students who have one to four pennies that they will receive a smaller reward (i.e., one extra point per penny). Those without any pennies receive nothing.

7. Ask again if there are any students in class who would like to give away any of their pennies to less wealthy classmates. Allow time for this to occur.

8. Tell students they will now have one last opportunity to redistribute the pennies if they wish to do so. Arrange the class into two groups: those who are satisfied with their wealth and those who are not. Ask each group to arrive at a plan for redistributing the pennies (i.e., all the wealth of the world). Announce that there will be ten minutes for discussion after which a vote will be taken.

9. Give each group a marker and sheet of paper (or chalk for the board). Tell each group to appoint a secretary to record their groups' plans. Also, ask each group to name their plan for easy identification during the final class discussion and vote.

10. Post the two plans prominently. Ask each secretary to read the group's plan and answer any questions

11. Take a vote; students who own five or more pennies have one vote. Penniless students have no vote. Tabulate the votes and announce which plan is to be implemented. Implement the plan and assign awards to students.

Debriefing

- How did you feel about the way in which the pennies were acquired and distributed?

- Were you treated fairly?

- Were there any students who gave pennies away? Why or why not?

- Was the game a fair and realistic portrayal of how wealth and power are distributed in the world?

- Would you have acted or voted as you did if the pennies had been one-dollar bills? $100 bills?

- After playing the game could you better identify with poor people? With wealthy people?

- Why were student votes distributed the way they were?

- What people in our society/community have little wealth/power?

- What people or nations in the world are poor? Wealthy?

- How many countries are "have nots?"

- How many "have" nations are there?

- Why should powerful countries be concerned about the have nots? Why would they give money to poor countries?

- How can goods and resources be equitably distributed?

Follow-up

1. Assign students to find magazine and newspaper articles about the global distribution of goods and resources, wealth and poverty.

2. Show a film about hunger or poverty in your country.

COMPARING COUNTRIES AND COMPANIES:
A CARD GAME

Introduction

This activity is designed to increase student awareness of the relative size of multinational corporations (MNCs) and their potential impact upon the global economic system. Students will play a card game which will enable them to compare annual sales figures for selected MNCs with gross national product figures (GNP) figures of certain industrialized and developing countries. Based on this data and their experience playing the game, students will make generalizations about the relative size and power of MNCs within the global economic system.

Objectives

Students will be able to:

- Become familiar with specific data from ten industrialized countries, ten developing countries, and ten selected MNCs.
- Compare gross national product figures of selected industrialized countries, GNP figures for certain developing countries, and net annual sales figures of certain MNCs.
- Critically analyze this data and formulate hypotheses about the relative size and power of MNCs within the global economic system.

Grade Level

10-12

Time

One class period

Materials

Handout #1, "Cards," copy for each pair of students
Handout #2, "Gross National Product"

Procedure

1. Divide the class into pairs.

2. Direct the students to shuffle cards and deal half the deck (fifteen cards) to each student.

3. Each player places the cards in a pile on the table with the names of the countries and companies facing upward. On the count of three both players take the top card from their piles and place them in the middle of the table, keeping the name side up. Students should guess which country/company is biggest. Countries are measured in terms of GNP figures and companies are measured in terms of gross annual sales figures. After guessing, students should turn the cards over to determine which is actually the largest. The largest figure wins. The student with the winning card takes the loser's card and puts both cards aside in a separate pile. Repeat this procedure for the remaining fourteen cards.

4. At the end of the round, shuffle the cards and instruct the students to play two more rounds.

5. Have the players count the cards in their piles. The player with the greatest number of cards is declared the winner.

6. Ask both winners and losers to lay their cards out in front of them. What observations/generalizations can be made about the types of cards in each pile? Are there any similarities between cards in the same piles? Are there any differences between piles? Where are the cards for the industrialized countries? The less developed countries? The MNCs?

7. Ask some of the pairs to share their generalizations with the class. Also ask students what observations they made playing the game. Did a specific pattern of play develop? Did anyone think that, in some cases, companies could win over countries?

8. Now tell the pairs to combine all the cards. Looking only at the figures for each country/company, instruct the students to rank order the cards 1-30, the highest figure being 1 and lowest figure being 30. Lay them out on a desk or a table.

9. Tell students to turn all the cards over to the name side, keeping them in their ranked position. Looking at the list of companies/countries, what new observations can be made when the cards are organized this way? Where are the industrialized countries located? The MNCs? The developing countries. Encourage students to share their ideas with the class.

10. Distribute Handout #2. Ask:

• What sort of information does this sheet provide?

• What observations can you make about the size of the GNP for North America and the European Economic Community?

• What percentage of the total do these two areas account for?

• Rearrange the data, rank ordering the groups of countries from the highest to the lowest, according to GNP values.

• Where does the figure for the top fifty U.S. MNCs in the world lie with respect to the other figures? What generalizations can you make from the data about the relative wealth and economic power of MNCs in the global economic system?

Debriefing

• Are there any problems in comparing a gross domestic product and gross annual revenue figures? What kind of information do these figures provide? What important considerations/-measurements are not included in this concept?

• What additional information might provide a better comparison between countries and companies?

- What other data might provide more information as to the size and power of global corporations?

- Can multinational corporations be regarded as factors that hold power and influence equal to that of the nation-state? Why or why not?

Follow-up Choose one multinational corporation and research such things as its operations, type of products produced, number of employees, and number of plants in nations other than the home country. Share this information with the class.

CARDS

1990 GNP IN MILLIONS OF U.S. DOLLARS 127,561	1990 GNP IN MILLIONS OF U.S. DOLLARS 2,847,854
1990 GNP IN MILLIONS OF U.S. DOLLARS 734,482	1990 GNP IN MILLIONS OF U.S. DOLLARS 7,135
1990 GNP IN MILLIONS OF U.S. DOLLARS 359,688	1990 GNP IN MILLIONS OF U.S. DOLLARS 5,123
1990 GNP IN MILLIONS OF U.S. DOLLARS 3,013	1990 GNP IN MILLIONS OF U.S. DOLLARS 2,080

JAPAN	CANADA
URUGUAY	UNITED KINGDOM
YEMEN	PEOPLE'S REPUBLIC OF CHINA
ZAMBIA	BAHRAIN

1990 GNP IN MILLIONS OF U.S. DOLLARS 164,700	1990 GNP IN MILLIONS OF U.S. DOLLARS 23,900
1990 GNP IN MILLIONS OF U.S. DOLLARS 6,530	1990 GNP IN MILLIONS OF U.S. DOLLARS 1,384,420
1990 GNP IN MILLIONS OF U.S. DOLLARS 58,865	1990 GNP IN MILLIONS OF U.S. DOLLARS 977,368
1990 GNP IN MILLIONS OF U.S. DOLLARS 38,666	1990 GNP IN MILLIONS OF U.S. DOLLARS 1,349

SWEDEN	LIBYA
GERMANY	ZIMBABWE
FRANCE	BELGIUM
LAOS	COLOMBIA

1990 GNP IN MILLIONS OF U.S. DOLLARS 194,709	1990 GNP IN MILLIONS OF U.S. DOLLARS 235,913
1990 GNP IN MILLIONS OF U.S. DOLLARS 4,250	1990 GNP IN MILLIONS OF U.S. DOLLARS 4,872,404
1992 NET ANNUAL REVENUE 781,000 MILLION	1992 NET ANNUAL REVENUE 746,000 MILLION
1992 NET ANNUAL REVENUE 6,119 MILLION	1992 NET ANNUAL INCOME 4,132 MILLION

14

THE NETHERLANDS	SWITZERLAND
PANAMA	USA
SEAGRAM CO LTD (CANADA)	ROYAL DUTCH/SHELL GROUP (THE NETHERLANDS UK)
PHILIPS ELECTRONICS (THE NETHERLANDS)	ELECTROLUX (SWEDEN)

1992 NET ANNUAL REVENUE 124,705 MILLION	1992 NET ANNUAL REVENUE 138,220 MILLION
1992 NET ANNUAL REVENUE 105,519 MILLION	1992 NET ANNUAL REVENUE 97,825 MILLION
1992 NET ANNUAL REVENUE 59 MILLION	1992 NET ANNUAL REVENUE 541.8 MILLION
1992 NET ANNUAL REVENUE 108,521 MILLION	1992 NET ANNUAL REVENUE 162.1 MILLION

GENERAL MOTORS (USA)	UNILEVER (THE NETHERLANDS/UK)
EXXON (USA)	NESTLE (SWITZERLAND)
HANSON INDUSTRIES (UK)	IBM (USA)
PETROLEOS de VENEZUELA (VENEZUELA)	FORD MOTOR (USA)

GROSS NATIONAL PRODUCTS

AREA	GNP/MILLIONS $
Africa	358,867
North America	5,300,471
Latin America and Caribbean	708,782
Middle East	464,844
East and Southeast Asia (Less Japan)	1,330,105
Japan	2,847,854
Western Europe	5,002,492
Asia Pacific	250,590
Top 50 U.S. MNCs (i.e., revenue)	1,452,371

Sivard, Ruth Leger. World Military and Social Expenditures 1993. Washington, D.C.: World Priorities, 1993, and Forbes, 7/18/94.

Introduction

Modernization and technological innovation exert subtle and profound effects on people's lives. In this exercise students become aware of modernization's effect on (or ramifications for) people's lifestyles and on the entire world.

Objectives

Students will be able to:

• Become aware of how modernization and new technology affect people's lifestyles and their environments.
• Explore strategies available for coping with sudden or profound changes in one's environment.
• Invent useful tools for people of different cultural backgrounds and lifestyles.
• Explore creative and flexible ways of adapting to modernization and technological change.

Grade Level

6-12

Time

One to two class periods

Materials

A set of at least twenty pictures of individuals from different cultures involved in different activities (e.g., coalminers in Wales or Wyoming, women business executives, farmers in Iowa, an old couple on a street corner, a rice farmer in Asia, or a factory worker in Hong Kong). Some good sources for pictures are National Geographic, Geo, Life, or Fortune magazines.
Legos, Tinker Toys, or Erector Set
Drawing materials
Handout #3, "Ramification Sheet"

Procedure

1. Briefly discuss with students the concept of change (to undergo transformation, transition, or substitution which implies making either an essential difference amounting to a loss of original identify, or a substitution of one thing for another). Ask students to brainstorm a list of changes that have occurred in our global society due to the introduction of a new technology (a method of achieving a practical purpose). For example: What were the effects of the invention of the automobile? What were the impacts of the introduction of the tractor in rural developing countries? What changes have occurred because of the former Soviet and U.S. space programs?

2. Distribute one picture to each student or small group of students. Ask them to develop a possible profile for the people in their pictures.

- In what country is this picture taken? Is it part of the developed, industrialized world (e.g., United States, Canada, Japan, Western Europe)? Or part of the industrializing or developing world (e.g., most of Africa, Asia, and Latin America)?

- What is the income of the persons in this picture? Base your figures on whether they live in developed or developing nations.

- What sort of food, shelter, education, employment, and leisure activities do the people in the picture have?

- Other issues that might be included in the profile: size of family, population of region, health facilities, weather, and so on. There are a number of resources available to help students develop their profiles.

- Work with your library or media resource center to locate materials dealing with the issues of development, food and hunger, population, global poverty, basic needs, and area studies. This part of the activity should provide the students an excellent chance to develop some research skills.

3. Have the students share their profiles with the entire class. You might have students discuss similarities and differences between the developed and developing areas as presented in their profiles.

4. Now, assign a "profound and significant change" to each student or group and ask them to introduce an appropriate method of coping with this change. The changes you might introduce include: a natural disaster, e.g., typhoon, hurricane, drought, or flood; a war or conflict with a neighboring country; the building of a factory in a rural town or the closing of a factory in an industrial area; a breakdown of the government; the introduction of a tractor in an agricultural community; or a population explosion. You might draw from the list that the students brainstormed at the beginning of the activity.

Students are to play the role of inventor and design and draw, or even build, a model of their invention that will help the persons in the pictures cope with the changes. Stress the need to be creative. In some cases an invention will not help and students should be made aware of the fact that often intangibles such as faith are the only responses to profound changes.

5. Have students share their methods of coping with the changes with the rest of the class. Discuss how different cultures respond to changes. Explore the possible effects of this invention on the society in which the people live. Have students list all of the possible ramifications for their profiles, using Handout #3, and compare with the others in the class.

Debriefing

- Were you able to empathize with the person for whom you invented something?

- How were the inventions in class similar? Different? Would you classify your invention as "high technology" or not? What about the inventions of others in class?

- Would you consider your invention an appropriate technology invention (appropriate for the problem and the lifestyle of the person)? Why? Are the other inventions appropriate or not?

- How realistic was your invention?

- What sort of impact would the invention have on the person's lifestyle?

- What sort of effect would the invention have upon the environment?

- How would the world change because of your invention? Because of other class inventions?

- How would the world change if all the inventions began to be used at the same time?

- Can all of society's problems be solved by technological innovation and implementation?

Follow-up

1. Have students make a list of things at school, home, or community they consider to be examples of inappropriate technology and tell why.

2. Have students research the ramification for society of important inventions: the chimney, the astrolab, the stirrup, the iron plow, the internal combustion engine. Make a chart showing all the different effects of change using Handout #3.

3. Have students research inventions that have been used in different cultures at different times, such as the calendar and gunpowder.

4. Have students list the most important technological developments that have occurred in their own lifetimes, the effects on themselves, and ramifications for the future.

5. Have students predict what problems may or may not be solved in their lifetime by technology. Predict problems that might occur because of the introduction of the inventions themselves.

RAMIFICATION SHEET

Picture Profile

Profound Change

Invention

Ramifications (impacts or effects) of your invention:

II. WORLDTRADE AND INTERDEPENDENCY

Introduction

Futurist Alvin Toffler, author of <u>Future Shock</u> and <u>Previews and Premises</u>, argues that our personal lives are insulated from what is happening in the world at large. Further, this isolation contributes to our refusal to recognize impending world catastrophes and to our unwillingness to accept responsibility for shaping world events.

Is Toffler correct? What are the implications of his statement for citizen participation in decision making in an age of increasing interdependence among nations? In this activity students consider their personal futures and formulate a scenario for the future of the world. They examine the relationship between their personal scenario and their vision of a future world, then consider the extent to which their actions will affect global events and vice versa.

Objectives

Students will be able to:

- Become aware of the complexity and interdependent nature of the world's political, economic, and social systems.
- Understand the relationship between students' personal lives and the global environment.
- Develop an awareness of how people's perceptions, values, and priorities differ.

Grade Level

6-12

Time

One class period

Materials

8 1/2" X 11" unlined paper
Pencils or markers

Procedure

1. Distribute paper. Ask each student to draw a ten-inch arrow on which to plot timelines of what they think their futures will be like. The timeline should begin at present. There need not be a definite end point. Ask students to predict five major events that will occur in their personal lives. They should describe these events, locate them on the timeline, and date them.

2. Ask students to predict five major global events they think will occur in their lifetimes. Have them describe these events, then locate and date them on the same timeline.

3. Draw a giant timeline on the chalkboard. Ask students to describe their personal scenarios. Mark some of their personal events on this timeline. What kinds of events did people predict they would experience? What similarities and differences exist among these predictions?

4. Ask students to share their global predictions. Add these events to the giant timeline. Ask students why they chose the events they named. Are their predictions optimistic or pessimistic? Why? What similarities and differences exist between these predictions?

Debriefing

- What, if any, points of congruence are there between your personal and global timelines?

- Are the two sets of predictions mutually exclusive? Explain.

- When we plan our personal lives, what do we take for granted about the world? What characteristics of our present global system can we assume will remain unchanged in our lifetimes?

- What skills will citizens need to deal with some of the changes outlined in your global scenario? How can people acquire these skills?

- Do you think your own future will be affected by what happens to the world during your lifetime? How?

- What are the consequences of ignoring our collective future at the expense of our individual futures? Explain your answer.

Follow-up

Develop a computerized timeline utilizing the program *TimeLiner*, available from CTIR. The program is from Tom Snyder Productions, Inc., and helps students to develop timelines of their own. Data disks are also available that contain predeveloped timelines that can then be merged with the students' own.

NUTS TO YOU!
A SIMULATION OF INTERNATIONAL PEANUT TRADE

Introduction

This simulation is designed to increase student awareness of the interconnectedness and complexity of our global food system. It illustrates the dynamics of international commodity trade and the political, economic, and social relationships that exist between the rich and the poor worldwide. By playing various roles in a number of hypothetical situations, students develop a greater understanding of how an ordinary agricultural product such as peanuts binds us to people in other lands.

Although this activity uses peanuts as an example of a primary product that is crucial to developed as well as underdeveloped nations, it can easily be adapted to illustrate global interdependence with regard to other commodities, i.e., oil, coffee, tea, cocoa, tin, and rubber. Films and readings for other commodity areas are listed at the end of this activity.

Objectives

Students will be able to:

*   Articulate what it feels like to be powerful or powerless in situations involving crucial global resources.
*   Describe several ways in which U.S. and Third World people are linked to the global economic system.
*   Discuss some of the reasons why the global economic system is interdependent.
*   Formulate hypotheses about why the global economic system benefits some countries and individuals at the expense of others.

Grade Level

8-12

Time

Two hours

Materials

Handout #4, "Actor Profile"
Handout #5, "Situations"
Supplemental films or readings (optional)

Procedure

1. Tell your class that this simulation demonstrates the ramifications of production and trade of a single agricultural product, peanuts, that is important worldwide. Explain that they will role play various situations concerning the production and sale of peanuts. Each student will be assigned a different role. In all, there are fourteen actor profiles. If there are more than fourteen students in your class, you may want to devise some system by which students can share roles.

2. Distribute an actor profile to each student and have them take turns reading them aloud. Ask students to think about what the goals and needs are of the people they portray. Have the class discuss the subject.

3. Explain that role playing is different than dramatic acting. The student role players need not be entertaining, but they should interact realistically. They should react to imaginary situations in a way in which they think their assigned characters would react.

4. Tell the class you will direct the simulation through the use of situations. Each one poses a different situation that might affect world peanut production and trade. Not all students will participate in role playing each situation.

5. Choose a situation and read it aloud to the class. Ask your students who would be involved in role playing that particular situation. One way to have all the characters interact might be to have the U.S. and British reporters interview the entire group concerning their reactions to the situation.

6. Allow students time to role play the situation you announced. Hold a short class discussion of the situation and the way in which it was role played. Was it acted realistically? What could cause the situation to change? How could the situation improve or get worse?

7. Repeat steps 5 and 6, using a new situation. There are ten, so the simulation can be played for up to ten rounds.

Debriefing

- What were the priorities of the different characters portrayed? How and why were these in conflict?

- Which characters were most powerful? Which were least powerful? Why? How did the powerful exercise control over the situations in which they were involved?

- How did the actions of the powerful affect the relatively powerless players?

- If you were one of the powerless players, what changes would you make in peanut production and trade that would be to your advantage?

- What obstacles prevented players from achieving their goals? Are there any similarities between poor laborers in Senegal and in the United States? What are the differences?

- Discuss the role of the news correspondents. How did they report each situation? How did their perceptions of various situations differ from those of other actors?

- What other agricultural commodities are grown, processed, and distributed worldwide? Who benefits from these crops? Of these people, who benefits the most? The least?

Follow-up   Ask students to construct a web chart that depicts the interrelationships among the actors, institutions, and the conditions involved in the role play. Construction of a web chart graphically illustrates the interdependent nature of the global food system and the political, economic, and social interconnections that exist between individuals in the United States and the developing world.

ACTOR PROFILES

You are the United States Secretary of Agriculture.	You are a CNN news correspondent researching a story on peanut farming in Senegal and the United States.
You are the Minister of Agriculture in Senegal.	You are the Senegalese Ambassador to the United States.
You are a news reporter from the BBC stationed in Senegal.	You are a young Peace Corps volunteer teaching school in a rural village outside of Dakar, Senegal.
You are the wife of a peanut farmer in Senegal. You were married when you were 15; now you are 25. You have 5 children, who are extremely ill and malnourished. You are malnourished yourself, yet you help your husband in the peanut fields as well as fulfilling your duties as wife and mother. You would like to buy you children some clothes and shoes, but there is no money. You realize that your children are suffering. You wonder why they cannot consume more of the peanut crop instead of growing the nuts for export.	You are a 42-year-old peanut farmer in Georgia. This farm has been in your family for 3 generations. You own over 500 acres of land and earn $400,000 per year. You also own 3 large harvester-combines valued at $100,000 each. You employ five uneducated black laborers on your farm; at harvest time you often employ additional (mostly black) workers and rent 1 or 2 more harvester-combines to aid the harvest. You are on the "up and up." Next year looks like it will be a very good year.

29

You are a peanut farmer in the African nation of Senegal. You own 20 acres of land 1 day's journey by oxcart from Dakar, the capital city. You have a wife and five young children. You, your brother and your wife work on the land using all hand tools. You live in a mud hut and eat mostly millet. Your children suffer from malnutrition yet they attend local school where they are taught by a young U.S. Peace Corps volunteer.	You are a senior official in the United States Agency for International Development (USAID). You have been informed that $1,500,000 worth of development funds for agricultural projects are available for Senegal. You have indicated this to Senegalese government officials and they have invited you to visit the country to see how these funds might be used. You complete an on-site inspection of peanut farming there and submit your suggestions to USAID.
You are the President of Planters Peanuts, Inc., the largest peanut processing company in the world. You buy peanuts from all over the world, but market them mostly in the United States. Your company is growing at an extremely rapid rate and you predict further growth for the next year.	You are a 50-year-old laborer employed on the peanut farm of a wealthy Georgia landowner. You have a wife and five children to support. You earn approximately $200 per week and live in the poorest section of a nearby town.
You are a United States Congressional Representative from Georgia. Your family has been involved in peanut farming in the state for 50 years. In fact you worked in the family peanut warehouse before you entered politics. Because you have been intimately associated with the economics of peanut farming you realize that protectionist policies and trade and tariff regulations are important if U.S. farmers are to have "crop security." You pride yourself on your "realist" and "Realistic" perceptions of the world.	You are the owner/manager of a peanut storage warehouse in Georgia. You buy peanuts from growers and sell them to large farms directly or indirectly, through a broker. In your "middleman" position you have been extremely successful, earning $33,000 per month.

30

SITUATIONS

Suddenly the Russians have fallen in love with peanut butter cookies. National consumption/demand is skyrocketing. The government officials, especially, cannot get enough.	The United States Congress passes a protective tariff on peanut imports.
Lack of sufficient rainfall all but destroys the annual peanut crop in Senegal. Domestic food supplies are extremely low.	The world market price of peanuts plummets.
There is a tremendous surplus of peanuts in the United States market. Reserves are at an all-time high.	Peasants riot in the streets of Dakar, denouncing the government's "developed" plan and the expense of goods and services.

Farm laborers on several of the largest plantations in Georgia wreck farm machinery in protest of their poor treatment and low wages.

Rodent infestation has become a major problem in the peanut storage facilities (built by USAID) in Dakar, Senegal. Thirty-five percent of the peanut crop is destroyed.

Planters Peanuts, Inc. opens a subsidiary in Dakar, Senegal.

The two youngest children of the Senegalese farmer die of malnutrition. The wife becomes ill with a high fever several days later and cannot work.

There is a severe drought in the southern portion of the United States which damages the peanut harvest severely.

International demand for peanut products continues to rise due to their promotion by UNESCO of nutritional value.

Introduction   By way of a simple simulation using a chocolate bar, students are introduced to the complexity and interdependent nature of the world's political, economic, and social systems.

Objectives   Students will be able to:

• Better understand the concept of global interdependence.
• Become more sensitive to the interrelationship between political, economic, and social factors and how they influence the price of goods we buy.

Grade Level   7-12

Time   Two to five class periods

Materials   Handout #6, "Role Sheets"
A candy bar

Procedure   1. Hold up a candy bar and ask the students to list the ingredients and identify and locate the country or countries of origin for those products; for example, chocolate from Brazil or Mexico.

2. Ask them to list factors which might influence the cost of the finished product; for example, transportation, weather, profit margins, demand/supply.

Explain to them that they will now participate in a simulation of trade policy-making which will influence the cost of that chocolate bar.

3. Divide the class into five groups and hand out role sheets for each group. As you hand them out, read the role sheet aloud so everyone knows the specifics of the entire situation.

      Team 1--Canadian Paper Industry
      Team 2--African Consortium for Agricultural Products
      Team 3--Iowa Farmers
      Team 4--Brazilian Chocolate Industries
      Team 5--The Candy Council

4. Have each team read its role sheets and discuss its policy choices. Each group should prepare a statement to be presented orally to The Candy Council. The Candy Council should discuss various alternatives. There is no need for intergroup communication, but it may be allowed for developing a strategy.

5. Have a spokesperson from each team present its new policy position to The Candy Council.

6. Give The Candy Council ten to fifteen minutes to decide on its policy and clarify the positions of other groups after which it will announce its decision and the new price of the chocolate bar.

Debriefing

- Discuss with students how this simple example of a chocolate bar demonstrates the interdependence of economics and politics.

- Have them discuss other consumer products such as automobiles, gas, oil, homes, etc.

- What are the implications of global interdependence for each of you as consumers in the world today?

ROLE SHEETS

Team #1: Canadian Paper Industry

Product: Paper for wrappers

The United States president has just announced in an executive order that a surcharge will be added to all of your paper products. This surcharge is designed to bring your prices in line with the cost of United States products.

Canadian paper now costs: $100 per ton + transportation
U.S. paper cost: $150 per ton + transportation
Surcharge: $ 50 per ton
(The surcharge will change as the U.S. paper price increases)

Approximately 11 percent of your business is with candy corporations selling in the U.S. These industries buy your paper because it is cheaper. Most likely they will now buy U.S. paper because with transportation costs your paper is now more expensive.

How will industry be affected? How will your industry adjust to this new price increase?

Can you think of any alternative markets or ways of continuing trade with the United States?

Report your findings to The Candy Council.

Team #2: African Consortium for Agricultural Products

Product: Peanuts

The United States administration, in an effort to support their country's businesses, placed restrictions on all countries that did not support their policies. Three of the four countries in your cartel do not support U.S. policies and the U.S. has cut off trade. Eighty percent of your trade is with U.S. food and candy manufacturers.

How will your consortium be affected?

How will you adjust to these restrictions?

Can you think of alternative marketing strategies?

Report your findings to The Candy Council.

Team #3: Iowa Farmers

Product: Corn syrup

Cargill Grain Corporation of Minnesota has just offered your farm co-op a higher price for your corn crop than you have been getting from the General Foods Corp., which manufactures corn syrup for the candy industry. Currently 80 percent of your trade is with General Foods and 20 percent with Cargill. Cargill plans to use the corn to produce gasahol and they plan to export about one-fourth of their supply to Russia. General Foods uses your corn for corn syrup and other foodstuffs which it exports throughout the world. You must decide whether to sell to Cargill or to General Foods.

Cargill price offer: $1.75 per bushel
General Foods price offer: 82 per bushel

Report your decision to The Candy Council.

36

Team #4: Brazilian Chocolate Industries

Product: Chocolate

You have had a bad year; drought has ruined most of your crops. Politics have also entered your industry. Germany has agreed to send your country nuclear power equipment, whereas the United States has refused. Your government, a military dictatorship, has strongly urged all industries to increase their trade to this European nation. Currently 70 percent of your trade is with the U.S., 20 percent with Europe, and 10 percent to other areas.

You must decide how you will export your product.

With the shortages, will you be forced to increase you prices?

Report your decision to The Candy Council.

Team #5: The Candy Council, made up of multinational food industries, e.g., General Foods, Nestle's, Beatrice, etc.

Each team will report its decision to your council. Your task is to respond to their policies by:

> Pulling out of the market, or
> Changing your prices, or
> Changing the product, or
> Diversification/expansion of your industry, or
> Finding alternative markets, or
> Other, specify _____

Because of your decision, how much will the final product, the candy bar, increase in price?

Will your decision impact other consumer areas?

Report your decision to the rest of the group.

| Introduction | Global interdependence manifests itself vividly in the complex matrices of international trade. By acting as members of the planetary business community, students will be able to grasp not only the concept of interdependence, but also some of its economic ramifications for the world's traders. |

Objectives

Students will be able to:

- Understand the ramifications of global interdependence in the sphere of international trade.
- . Conceptualize some effects of the maldistribution of goods and resources in the world.
- Understand some fundamental relationships of economics such as monopoly, oligopoly, and free trade.
- Develop strategies that successfully deal with the relationships between developed and less developed nations.

Grade Level

7-12

Time

One to two class periods

Materials

Handout #7, "Going After Mr Goodbar Rules"
Play money (Monopoly)
Pencil, pen, and paper
Bag of peanuts
Bag of chocolate kisses
Poker chips
Bag of miniature candy bars (Mr. Goodbar)
Ziplock sandwich bags
Bell

Procedure

1. Prior to class arrange "resources" by bag (for a class of thirty)
   15 bags of 10 peanuts/no chocolate/no poker chips/no money
   10 bags of 0, 1, 2, or 3 peanuts/5-10 chocolate kisses/no poker chips/$100-$500
   4 bags of $1,000/10-15 poker chips/3-5 peanuts
   1 bag of $1,600/15 poker chips/10 peanuts

2. Distribute bags among students.

3. As the director, you are responsible for timing ten to fifteen minute rounds; selling candy bars, poker chips; providing new "harvest" of peanuts; and keeping a lid on the action. (Assistant directors may be necessary for larger classes.)

Originally in <u>Comparative World Issues for Grades 1-12</u>, CTIR, 1981; written by Roger Myers.

4. Directions to students:

Each of you is now equipped to be a business person operating on a global scale. Each of you has the capability to achieve success. Good and bad luck figure into your success equation, but so does your skill. Your GOAL is to manufacture as many candy bars as you can during the course of the games.

In order to manufacture candy you need one chocolate kiss, one peanut, capital (i.e., money) to begin your industry, and the technology capable of manufacturing a complicated product like candy (represented by the poker chip).

The bag in front of you will start you in business. As in the real world, not all of you will immediately have all the necessary ingredients. You will have to trade for them or buy from someone else. There are no set prices for any goods. All trading will close when you hear the bell.

Debriefing

- What strategy did you employ during the game? Was it successful?

- Does the game represent the real world of international trade faithfully? In what ways?

- In what ways does the game diverge from what really goes on in the international market place?

- How can the poor countries/business people survive?

- What sorts of incentives or aims helped you during the game?

- Who was the most successful and why?

GOING AFTER MR. GOODBAR RULES

1. To make a candy bar you need:
   1 peanut + 1 chocolate kiss + 1 poker chip + $500

2. At the end of a round, if you have the ingredients, you will trade them to the director for a candy bar.

3. You may keep the candy bar, or sell it to the director for $1,000, or for 1 poker chip and $500.

4. You may receive x number of peanuts at the end of each round.
   You may receive y number of kisses at the end of each round.

5. Poker chips (technology) will preserve peanuts for 1 round, chocolate for 2 rounds.

6. You can purchase a poker chip for $500 at the end of a round.

7. Record transactions below:

Rounds:	Peanuts	Chocolate	Money	Poker Chips	Candy Bar
Begin With:					
Round 1					
Round 2					
Round 3					
Round 4					
Round 5					
Round 6					
Round 7					

Introduction

This game is an excellent way for students to experience some of the bargaining processes that decision makers must consider when dealing with other nations. "World Trade" serves as an excellent introduction to the dynamics of international trade.

Objectives

Students will be able to:

- Better understand the world as an interdependent system.
- To learn decision-making skills needed for trading for different commodities.
- Understand the implications and results of various bargaining strategies.

Grade Level

6-12

Time

Two to four class periods

Materials

Five construction paper signs labeled Agria, Industria, Consumia, Mineria, and Energia
Handout #8, "World Trade Rules"
Handout #9, "Score Sheet"

Procedures

1. Tell your students that the game "World Trade" is not a replica of the current international trade system. Its purpose is to help students understand that business decisions are not made in a vacuum, but result from the pressures and perspectives that form the trade system in which nations operate.

2. Divide the class into five groups and distribute a sign to each group.

3. Distribute and read Handout #8. Answer any questions students may ask regarding procedures.

4. Distribute Handout #9. Ask students to discuss which policy they wish to follow during the first round. Each group must unanimously agree on a policy. Failure to agree means an automatic loss of 100 points. The groups should keep their plans secret from one another. There will be no intergroup communication during the first five rounds.

5. Ask each group to pass you a slip of paper announcing its policy decision. When all five have handed in their notes, mark the decisions on the chalkboard and award each nation its points. Then request that the groups quietly discuss second round strategy.

6. Play the second round. Then have students play three more rounds without communication among groups.

7. After the fifth round tell students they will be able to send a one-minute message to other nations through the International Radio. Nations are not required to speak if they do not desire to do so. Give them five minutes to decide what they will say. After the broadcasts, proceed to round six. Repeat this communication session each round thereafter.

8. The following incidents can be announced as needed:

- Bad weather will cost Agria 50 points. All other nations receive 20 points.

- World slump in demand for consumer products. Consumia loses 50 points.

- New technological invention makes some industrial plants in Industria obsolete. Industria loses 50 points.

- Development of solar power destroys market for energy. Energia loses 100 points.

- Mineria exhausts some natural resources. Mineria loses 50 points.

- World population outstrips economic development. All nations lose 50 points.

- World economic recession. All nations lose 50 points. If at least four nations do not choose Policy A, all nations will again lose 50 points in the next round.

9. Note on Revolutions: Nations are subject to revolution every time their cumulative score falls below -300. You may declare revolutions at your discretion. After a nation has a revolution, explain that other nations with more than 300 points may give that country some of their points as foreign aid.

Debriefing

- Give a brief narrative history of the simulation. (As other students offer different interpretations of the history of the simulation, get them to speculate why their interpretations differ.) Is it different roles? Different vantage points?

- How does what you did in this simulation resemble trade in the real world? Were there parts that did not resemble trade as you see it?

Follow-up

Once students have played the game and you have discussed what happened and why, students could research the actual trade policies of nations to see how they compare to their behavior in the game. Have students try to rewrite the pay-offs to change the behavior of the participants to a more cooperative system. Ask students what would have to happen to make the international trade system a more cooperative venture.

WORLD TRADE RULES

You are about to play a simulation. The simulated world consists of five fictitious groups of nations:

Agria: Has a large surplus of agricultural products, but must import other products to survive.
Industria: Produces heavy industrial products, but must import other products to survive.
Consumia: Produces consumer products, but must import other products to survive.
Energia: Produces energy, but must import other products to survive.
Mineria: Produces mineral resources, but must import other products to survive.

Your group must decide whether it will follow:

Policy A.   Encourage trade by a combination of lowered tariffs and lowered exported goods prices;
Policy B.   Keep trade barriers at current levels and maintain prices of exported products; or
Policy C.   Increase cost of major export products and/or create higher tariff levels.

If all nations encourage trade by selecting choice A, all nations will benefit from the increased trade.

If all nations choose Policy C, trade will decrease, hence all nations will lose.

The following points will accrue to nations when the indicated mixed situations occur:

POLICY	A	B	C
No nations choose C	+100	+30	-0-
1 nation chooses C	+20	+10	+100
2 nations choose C	-10	-0-	+50
3 nations choose C	-50	-20	-0-
4 nations choose C	-100	-50	-50
5 nations choose C	-0-	-0-	

All nations can survive some negative points. However, any nation with a cumulative score below -300 is subject to internal revolution. Revolutions are costly and nation loses an additional 100 points.

SCORE SHEET

Group _____

	CHOICES					YOUR POINTS
	Agria	Energia	Mineria	Consumia	Industria	
1.						
2.						
3.						
4.						
5.						
6.						
7.						
8.						
9.						
10.						
					TOTAL	

Introduction

This activity is designed to increase student awareness of the different types of multinational corporations (MNCs) and their sizes, structures, and financial profiles. Students will examine two charts, "Multinationals" and "Foreign Investments." By analyzing this information they will develop a greater understanding of the depth and scope of multinational investment abroad and in the United States.

Objectives

Students will be able to:

• Develop a greater awareness of the different types of multinational companies.
• Acquire, analyze, and use data to develop a greater awareness of the size, structure, and financial profile of these different multinational corporations.
• Discover the nature and extent to which we utilize the products/services of MNCs in our everyday life.
• Become aware of the extent to which United States multinationals invest abroad and of the nature and extent of foreign investment in the United States.

Grade Level

10-12

Time

One or two class periods

Materials

Handout #10, "Multinationals"
Handout #11, "Foreign Investments"

Procedure

1. Divide the class into groups. Distribute Handout #10.

2. Discuss the terms "revenue," "net profit," and "assets." Explain the meaning of each column in the charts. With regard to the largest U.S. multinationals ask:

• How many companies on this chart do you recognize? Go through the list and put a check beside each one.

• Can you recognize the products/services available from each company? List as many as you can for each global company with which you are familiar.

• How many of the items you have listed are essential to your way of life?

• What items do you use most often as an individual?

• What items do we use most often as a society?

- Does the rest of the world have a similar pattern of consumption?

- What types of companies are represented on this list? Group them according to type (e.g., bank, oil, auto, or food). Which types are most prevalent? Why?

- Which companies have the largest total revenue? List the top fifteen.

- Make a list of the fifteen companies with the largest amount of foreign revenue. Are they the same corporations as you listed above?

- Do the companies which receive the largest percentage of their profits outside the United States (Column 6) receive a similar percentage of their total revenue from foreign investments (Column 3)? Why would these two figures be different? Explain.

- Which company do you suppose has overseas investments in the greatest number of foreign nations? In what countries do you think the top ten have investments? Be able to support your answer.

3. Distribute Handout #11.

4. Have the students consider these questions with regard to largest foreign investments:

- At first glance, what, if anything, surprises you about this chart?

- Go through the listings of United States companies (Column 3). Make a check (√) next to the companies of which you have heard. Make an "X" next to the companies whose products/services you use. Did you know that these companies were totally owned by larger corporations located outside the United States?

- Why is the subsidiary investment structure (the model of larger companies owning smaller companies) often adopted by multinational corporations?

- What advantages/disadvantages do you suppose this structure has with regard to taxes in the nation of the parent company? Taxes in the United States? The flow of revenue between the parent company and the subsidiary? Prices and convenience for the consumer in the parent nation and in the United States? Accountability and the necessity to abide by government business regulations in the United States? Profits for the parent company?

- What are the implications of this model of multinational investment for governments around the world? For consumers? What are the effects of this structure on the free market system? On local businesses in the United States and abroad? Do you think this investment structure is a good one? Why or why not?

- What are the implications of increasing amounts of foreign investment in the United States economy? Which industries in the United States have been most affected by foreign investment?

Follow-up

1. Have students research a multinational corporation of their choice. Instruct them to write the corporation asking for annual reports, shareholder profile statements, and other pertinent information such as advertising policies or extent of overseas operations. Have them interview members of the community who work for the company. They can write up a multinational corporate profile and present it to the class. If their corporation is involved in food or agribusiness, they might consult The Directory of Major U.S. Corporations Involved in Agribusiness and The Standard Directory of Advertisers.

2. Have students make a list of the major fast food chains they use and research what multinational corporation owns or controls them. Have a class discussion. What does the trend toward fast food eating and this investment model mean for the structure of the family, the quality of diets, and consumer control over fast food?

MULTINATIONALS

Aside from a few Marxist/Leninist stragglers, no one in the developing countries yells "Yanqui go home!" to U.S. multinational corporations anymore. Instead it's more likely: "Hey, how about investing some capital and know-how our way!"

Last year aggregate foreign sales of the 100 largest U.S.-based multinationals totaled $703 billion. For the eighth straight year, the top five companies on our list were Exxon, General Motors, Mobil, IBM and Ford Motor. But don't think these five will always be there. Last year their aggregate foreign sales fell by $14 billion. Much of the shock was taken up by new U.S. technology leaders that are thrusting into overseas markets--Compaq Computer, for example, and Intel. Both made strong sales gains in Europe.

Along with computers and communications companies, America's makers and marketers of consumer branded goods are benefiting from a craze for things American. In soft drinks and snack foods, for example, Coca-Cola improved foreign sales by 7% last year, while PepsiCo showed a 24% gain. And in consumer products, Gillette was up 2%.

Another growth area for U.S. multinationals: financial services. American International Group, the insurance colossus, and Bank of Boston each generated over $1 billion of new revenues abroad last year. And look at Merrill Lynch, which is underwriting European equity privatizations, Euromarket debt issues and derivative products. One year ago Merrill Lynch failed to make our list. Now it is ranked number 45, with an estimated $4.2 billion in foreign revenue.

--Brian Zajac

1993 Rank	Company	Revenue			Net profit[1]			Assets		
		foreign ($mil)	total ($mil)	foreign as % of total	foreign ($mil)	total ($mil)	foreign as % of total	foreign ($mil)	total ($mil)	foreign as % of total
1	Exxon	75,639	97,825	77.3	4,066	5,280	77.0	47,445	84,145	56.4
2	General Motors	38,646	138,220	28.0	2,244	2,466	91.0	40,145	188,034	21.3
3	Mobil	38,535	57,077	67.5	1,917	2,401	79.8	25,420	40,585	62.6
4	IBM	37,013	62,716	59.0	-2,389	-7,987	D-D	44,703	81,113	55.1
5	Ford Motor	32,860	108,521	30.3	-293	2,529	D-P	51,669	198,938	26.0
6	Texaco	24,292	45,395	53.5	760	1,468	51.8	11,895	30,410	39.1
7	Citicorp	20,762	32,196	64.5	1,560	1,919	81.3	117,123	228,240	51.3
8	El du Pont de Nemours	16,756	32,621	51.4	565	566	99.8	13,807	37,053	37.3
9	Chevron	16,601	40,352	41.1	848	1,265	67.0	20,541	37,223	55.2
10	Procter & Gamble	15,856	30,433	52.1	175	269	65.1	10,157	24,935	40.7
11	Philip Morris Cos	15,315	50,621	30.3	1,278	3,568	35.8	15,619	51,205	30.5
12	Hewlett-Packard	10,971	20,317	54.0	675	1,177	57.3	7,508	16,736	44.9
13	American Intl Group	10,148	20,135	50.4	1,034	1,918	53.9	36,532	101,015	36.2
14	General Electric	10,036	60,562	16.6	323	4,424	7.3	31,791	251,506	12.6
15	Coca-Cola	9,351	13,957	67.0	1,484	2,188	67.8	5,844	12,021	48.6
16	Xerox	9,242	19,434	47.6	141	-189	P-D	10,119	39,677	25.5
17	Digital Equipment	9,152	14,371	63.7	114	-251	P-D	6,641	10,950	60.6
18	Dow Chemical	8,775	18,060	48.6	279	919	30.4	10,602	25,505	41.6
19	United Technologies	8,148	21,081	38.7	365	573	63.7	4,403	15,618	28.2
20	Eastman Kodak	7,980	16,364	48.8	197	475	41.5	6,588	20,325	32.4
21	Motorola	7,450E	16,963	43.9	867	1,022	84.8	4,674	13,498	34.6
22	ITT	7,411	22,762	32.6	233	937	24.9	7,318	70,560	10.4
23	Johnson & Johnson	6,935	14,138	49.1	975	1,787	54.6	5,380	12,242	43.9
24	Minn Mining & Mfg	6,894	14,020	49.2	338	1,295	26.1	4,874	12,197	40.0
25	PepsiCo	6,712	25,021	26.8	607	1,588	38.2	6,922	23,706	29.2
26	JP Morgan & Co	6,255	11,941	52.4	1,191	1,723	69.1	60,522	133,888	45.2
27	Chrysler	5,753	43,600	13.2	447	2,415	18.5	6,205	43,830	14.2
28	Amoco	5,740	25,793	22.3	552	1,820	30.3	8,454	28,486	29.7
29	AT&T	5,576	67,156	8.3	170	3,974	4.3	6,901	60,766	11.4
30	UAL	5,560	14,511	38.3	NA	-31	NA	NA	12,840	NA
31	Chase Manhattan	5,545	11,417	48.6	861	466	184.8	30,460	102,103	29.8
32	Sara Lee	5,172	14,580	35.5	291	704	41.3	4,893	10,862	45.0
33	Bank of Boston	4,962	7,396	67.1	79	275	28.7	9,386	40,588	23.1
34	Goodyear Tire & Rubber	4,866	11,643	41.8	200	489	40.9	3,226	8,436	38.2
35	Bankers Trust New York	4,858	7,800	62.3	865	1,070	80.8	47,804	92,082	51.9
36	Bristol-Myers Squibb	4,686	11,413	41.1	662	1,959	33.8	2,980	12,101	24.6
37	Colgate-Palmolive	4,608	7,141	64.5	367	548	67.0	2,700	5,761	46.9
38	Merck	4,584	10,498	43.7	707	3,085	22.9	3,545	19,928	17.8
39	Atlantic Richfield	4,373	17,189	25.4	77	269	28.6	5,166	23,894	21.6
40	Intel	4,366	8,782	49.7	839	2,295	36.6	2,192	11,344	19.3

[1] From continuing operations or affiliates [2] Average assets [3] Includes other income [4] Excludes Canadian operations [5] Net income before corporate expense. [6] Net income before minority interest [7] Includes proportionate interest in unconsolidated subsidiaries [8] Operating profit. [9] Pretax income D-D: Deficit to deficit D-P: Deficit to profit P-D: Profit to deficit E: Estimate NA: Not available

©CTIR
University of Denver

1993 Rank	Company	Revenue foreign ($mil)	Revenue total ($mil)	Revenue foreign as % of total	Net profit[1] foreign ($mil)	Net profit total ($mil)	Net profit foreign as % of total	Assets foreign ($mil)	Assets total ($mil)	Assets foreign as % of total
41	Salomon	4,361	8,799	49.6	853	864	98.7	78,100	184,835	42.3
42	CPC International	4,326	6,738	64.2	275[7]	474[7]	58.0	3,289	5,061	65.0
43	RJR Nabisco	4,200E	15,104	27.8	280[a]	111[a]	252.3	4,031	31,295	12.9
44	American Express	4,180	14,173	29.5	465	1,605	29.0	19,124	94,132	20.3
45	Merrill Lynch	4,150E	16,588	25.0	702	1,394	50.4	51,311	152,910	33.6
46	Aflac	4,127	5,001	82.5	217	244	88.9	13,656	15,443	88.4
47	Woolworth	4,028	9,626	41.8	-171	-495	D-D	2,084	4,593	45.4
48	AMR	3,909	15,816	24.7	NA	-96	NA	NA	19,326	NA
49	Alcoa	3,777	9,056	41.7	435[7]	201[7]	216.4	4,996	11,597	43.1
50	Unisys	3,670	7,743	47.4	115	362	31.8	1,339	7,519	17.8
51	American Brands	3,667	8,288	44.2	406	668	60.8	3,986	16,339	24.4
52	Gillette	3,651	5,411	67.5	262	427	61.4	3,353	5,102	65.7
53	Apple Computer	3,589	7,977	45.0	357	87	410.3	1,773	5,171	34.3
54	Sears, Roebuck	3,550	50,838	7.0	8	2,409	0.3	2,691	90,808	3.0
55	Compaq Computer	3,521[a]	7,191	45.0	294	462	63.6	1,652[a]	4,084	40.5
56	McDonald's	3,477	7,408	46.9	488	1,083	45.1	5,650	12,035	46.9
57	Pfizer	3,472	7,478	46.4	275[7]	660[7]	41.7	3,755	9,331	40.2
58	Safeway	3,459	15,715	22.7	11	123	D-P	991	5,075	15.5
59	Chemical Banking	3,394	12,427	27.3	576	1,569	36.7	35,355	149,888	23.6
60	Kmart[a]	3,380	37,312	9.1	NA	-378	NA	NA	17,867	NA
61	Tenneco	3,367	13,255	25.4	178	451	39.5	3,489	15,373	22.7
62	Texas Instruments	3,209	8,523	37.7	NA	476	NA	2,249	5,993	37.5
63	Abbott Laboratories	3,061	8,408	36.4	766	1,399	20.4	2,027	7,689	26.4
64	HJ Heinz	3,053	7,103	43.0	292	530	55.1	2,891	6,821	42.4
65	Warner-Lambert	3,047	5,794	52.6	199	285	69.8	2,235	4,828	46.3
66	Rhone-Poulenc Rorer	2,900	4,019	72.2	201	421	47.7	2,564	4,050	63.8
67	International Paper	2,860E	13,685	20.9	-53	289	D-P	4,332	16,631	26.0
68	BankAmerica	2,847	15,900	17.9	538	1,954	27.5	31,465	186,933	16.8
69	Cigna	2,821	18,402	15.3	-17	234	D-P	8,945	84,975	10.5
70	Monsanto	2,740	7,902	34.7	115	494	23.3	2,685	8,640	31.1
71	American Home Products	2,609	8,305	31.4	292	1,469	19.9	1,951	7,687	25.4
72	AlliedSignal	2,607	11,827	22.0	86	656	13.1	2,186	10,829	20.2
73	Emerson Electric	2,606	8,174	31.9	170	708	24.0	2,719	7,814	34.8
74	Ralston-Purina Group	2,593	5,915	43.8	76	284	26.8	1,588	4,294	37.0
75	Delta Air Lines	2,580	11,997	21.5	NA	-415	NA	NA	11,871	NA
76	Archer Daniels Midland	2,545	9,811	25.9	22[a]	738[a]	3.0	925	8,404	11.0
77	Halliburton	2,533[7]	6,351[7]	35.9	-117[7]	-163[7]	D-D	1,787	5,403	33.1
78	Kellogg	2,512	6,295	35.9	229	681	33.6	1,789	4,237	42.2
79	Kimberly-Clark[a]	2,499	7,647	32.7	78	511	15.3	2,553	6,731	37.9
80	GTE	2,482	19,748	12.6	371	990	37.5	6,096	41,575	14.7
81	Eli Lilly	2,471	6,452	38.3	269	491	54.8	2,890	9,624	30.0
82	Avon Products	2,449	4,008	61.1	154[7]	257[7]	59.9	946	1,958	48.3
83	Whirlpool	2,410[a]	7,533	32.0	107[7]	243[7]	44.0	1,758[a]	6,047	29.1
84	TRW	2,305	7,548	29.0	-17	220	D-P	1,508	5,336	28.3
85	Caterpillar	2,301	11,615	19.8	46[a]	626[a]	7.3	2,535	14,807	17.1
86	Baxter International	2,298	8,879	25.9	206	-268	P-D	1,929	10,545	18.3
87	Price/Costco	2,297	15,498	14.8	44[a]	399[a]	11.0	485	3,940	12.3
88	Fluor	2,222	7,850	28.3	60	167	35.9	327	2,589	12.6
89	Time Warner[a]	2,167	14,544	14.9	-19	-164	D-D	2,564	29,467	8.7
90	Federal Express	2,140	7,808	27.4	-182[a]	377[a]	D-P	1,360	5,793	23.5
91	Deere & Co	2,119	7,694	27.5	-117	184	D-P	1,879	11,352	16.6
92	Manpower	2,112	3,180	66.4	40[a]	94[a]	42.6	599	833	71.9
93	Honeywell	2,068	5,963	34.7	120	322	37.3	1,469	4,598	31.9
94	Schering-Plough	2,056	4,341	47.4	365	825	44.2	1,422	4,317	32.9
95	Rockwell International	2,039[a]	10,840	18.8	95	562	16.9	1,846[a]	9,885	18.7
96	Quaker Oats	2,025	5,731	35.3	51	287	17.8	850	2,816	30.2
97	Sun Microsystems	1,988	4,309	46.1	60	157	38.2	1,187	2,768	42.9
98	Phillips Petroleum	1,975	12,309	16.0	204	245	83.3	2,305	10,868	21.2
99	AMP	1,960	3,451	56.8	118	297	39.7	1,499	3,118	48.1
100	Campbell Soup	1,930E	6,586	29.3	-128	257	D-P	2,211	4,898	45.1

[1]From continuing operations or affiliates. [2]Includes other income. [3]Net income before corporate expense. [4]Includes proportionate interest in unconsolidated subsidiaries. [5]Average assets [6]Excludes Canadian operations. [7]Net income before minority interest [8]Operating profit. [9]Pretax income. D-D Deficit to deficit D-P Deficit to profit P-D Profit to deficit E Estimate NA Not available

FOREIGN INVESTMENTS

A year for the record books

While the Clinton Administration talked down the dollar last year, foreigners were lapping them up. Last year foreigners bought a record $231 billion more U.S. assets than they sold. That net foreign investment figure is 57% ahead of 1992. Foreign investors were financing the U.S. trade deficit and a good part of the budget deficit as well.

Of last year's total, $158 billion was for financial assets, mostly Treasurys and corporate debt. But foreign firms more than doubled their investments in U.S. plant and equipment to $21 billion.

Britain's Hanson Plc. made the biggest purchase: $3.3 billion for Quantum Chemical. And Canada's Seagram

Co. Ltd. acquired an 8% interest in Time Warner. This year Seagram raised its stake to 15%. (Note: Time Warner isn't listed as one of Seagram's holdings in our table because the stake is below 20%, our threshold for inclusion.)

If 1993 was big for foreign buying of U.S. assets, 1994 will probably be even bigger. For example, in March MCI shareholders approved a $4.3 billion deal in which British Telecom will acquire 20% of MCI Communications.

This inflow of foreign money carries a danger, too—a danger that reared its ugly head late last month when the dollar sank to record lows against the Japanese yen. The danger: What flows in can also flow out.– GUSTAVO LOMBO

1993 rank	Foreign investor	Country	US investment	% owned	Industry	Revenue ($mil)	Net income ($mil)	Assets ($mil)
1	Seagram Co Ltd*	Canada	EI du Pont de Nemours*	24	chemicals, energy	32,732	566 0	37,053
			JE Seagram	100	beverages	3,784	180 0	9,182
						36,516		
2	Royal Dutch/Shell Group*	Netherlands/UK	Shell Oil	100	energy, chemicals	20,853	781 0	26,851
3	British Petroleum*	UK	BP America	100	energy	16,006	NA	18,293
4	Sony Corp*	Japan	Sony Music Entertainment	100	music entertainment			
			Sony Picture Entertainment	100	movies	12,195	NA	12,657
			Sony Electronics	100	consumer electronics			
5	Grand Metropolitan*	UK	Burger King	100	fast food	5,250		
			Pillsbury	100	food processing	3,700		
			Heublein	100	wines and spirits	1,600	NA	6,131
			Pearle Vision	100	eye care retailing	600		
			Other companies	100	wines and spirits	625		
						11,775		
6	Hanson*	UK	Hanson Industries	100	mining, aggregates, chemicals	7,975	758.6	18,700
			Quantum Chemical	100	petrochemicals	2,294	−222 5	4,980
			Smith Corona*	48	office supplies	309	−9 0	198
			Ground Round Restaurants*	33	restaurant chain	233	5.3	152
			Marine Harvest International*	27	food processing	137	9 4	104
						10,948		
7	Tengelmann Group	Germany	Great A&P Tea*	53	supermarkets	10,384	4 0	3,099
8	Nestle*	Switzerland	Nestle USA	100	food processing	8,646	NA	NA
			Alcon Laboratories	100	pharmaceuticals			
	L'Oreal*	France	Cosmair	>50	cosmetics	1 347	NA	NA
						9,993		
9	B.A.T Industries*	UK	Brown & Williamson Tobacco	100	tobacco	2,774	NA	NA
			Farmers Group	100	insurance	1 709	508 5	6,999
	Imasco	Canada	Hardee's Food Systems	100	fast food	4,957	NA	843
						9 440		
10	Toyota Motor Corp*	Japan	Toyota Motor Mfg	100	automotive	4,000E	NA	NA
			New United Motor Mfg	50	automotive	3,600E	NA	NA
	Nippondenso*	Japan	Nippondenso America	100	auto parts	1,800	NA	NA
						9,400		
11	Petroleos de Venezuela	Venezuela	Citgo Petroleum	100	refining, marketing	9,107	162 1	3,866
12	Unilever NV*	Netherlands	Unilever United States	100	food processing, personal prods	8,970	NA	8,560
	Unilever Plc*	UK						

* Publicly traded in the U S in shares or ADRs Note Some foreign investors on the list own U.S. companies indirectly through companies in italics.
E Estimate. NA Not available.

Reprinted with permission by <u>Forbes</u> July 18, 1994.

©CTIR
University of Denver

1993 rank	Foreign investor	Country	US investment	% owned	Industry	Revenue ($mil)	Net income ($mil)	Assets ($mil)
13	Delhaize "Le Lion"	Belgium	Food Lion*	25	supermarkets	7,610	3.9	2,504
14	Ahold*	Netherlands	First National Supermarkets	100	supermarkets	2,158		
			BI-LO	100	supermarkets	1,828		
			Tops Markets	100	supermarkets	1,565	NA	2,137
			Giant Food Stores	100	supermarkets	1,133		
			Red Food Stores	100	supermarkets	585	NA	NA
						7,269		
15	Philips Electronics NV*	Netherlands	Philips Electronics NA	100	electronics	5,955	136.1	3,028
			Whittle Communications LP	25	publishing	250E	NA	NA
	PolyGram NV*	Netherlands	PolyGram Records	100	music	909	NA	NA
						7,114		
16	Hoechst AG*	Germany	Hoechst Celanese	100	chemicals	6,899	101.0	7,917
17	Siemens AG*	Germany	Siemens Corp	100	electronics	5,579	-163.0	NA
			Osram Sylvania	100	lighting products	958	-5.6	NA
						6,537		
18	AXA	France	Equitable Cos*	49	insurance	6,480	234.5	98,991
19	Bayer*	Germany	Miles	100	chemicals, health care	6,459	131.7	5,242
20	Matsushita Electric Industrial*	Japan	Matsushita Elec Corp (Am)	100	electronics	2,200	NA	1,000
			MCA	100	entertainment	4,100	NA	NA
						6,300		
21	Rhone-Poulenc SA*	France	Rhone-Poulenc Rorer*	68	pharmaceuticals	4,019	421.1	4,050
			Rhone-Poulenc Inc	100	chemicals	2,236	NA	3,400
						6,255		
22	Franz Haniel & Cie	Germany	Scrivner	100	food distribution	6,000	NA	1,400
22	Honda Motor Co*	Japan	Honda of America Mfg	100	automotive	6,000E	NA	NA
24	Ito-Yokado*	Japan	Southland*	64	convenience stores	5,781	-11.3	1,999
	Seven-Eleven Japan*	Japan						
25	ASEA AB*	Sweden						
	BBC Brown Boveri*	Switzerland						
	ABB Asea Brown Boveri	Switzerland	Asea Brown Boveri	100	electrical equipment	5,600	NA	4,200
26	Pechiney SA	France	Pechiney Sales	100	aluminum	359	NA	294
	Pechiney International	France	American National Can	100	packaging	4,142		
			Howmet	100	gas turbines	777	NA	6,240
			Other companies	100	metals distribution	89		
						5,367		
27	BASF AG*	Germany	BASF Corp	100	chemicals, plastics	5,202	410.6	4,366
28	SmithKline Beecham Plc*	UK	SmithKline Beecham Corp	100	drugs, consumer prods	5,028	881.0	6,080
			Diversified Pharmaceutical Svcs	100	pharmaceutical services	142	26.0	69
						5,170		
29	Bridgestone*	Japan	Bridgestone/Firestone	100	tire, rubber	5,100	6.0	NA
30	News Corp*	Australia	News America	100	media, publishing	5,081	NA	9,758
31	Nissan Motor Co*	Japan	Nissan Motor Mfg USA	100	automotive	4,700E	NA	NA
32	Ciba-Geigy Ltd*	Switzerland	Ciba-Geigy Corp	100	chemicals, drugs	4,600	NA	4,030
33	Electrolux*	Sweden	White Consolidated Inds	100	appliances	4,496	NA	NA
34	Northern Telecom Ltd*	Canada	Northern Telecom Inc	100	telecommunications	4,431	NA	4,020
35	Allianz AG	Germany	Fireman's Fund	100	insurance	3,300	280.0	9,800
			Allianz Life	100	insurance	865	84.0	9,779
			Allianz Insurance	100	insurance	137	27.0	1,109
			Jefferson Insurance	100	insurance	86	9.0	327
						4,388		

* Publicly traded in the U.S. in shares or ADRs. Note: Some foreign investors on the list own U.S. companies indirectly through companies in italics.
E: Estimate.   NA: Not available.

51

1993 rank	Foreign investor	Country	US investment	% owned	Industry	Revenue ($mil)	Net income ($mil)	Assets ($mil)
36	Henkel KGaA	Germany	Clorox*	28	household products	1,634	167.1	1,649
			Ecolab*	24	institutional cleaning	1,042	75.9	863
			Henkel of America	100	chemicals	1,009	NA	NA
			Loctite*	30	chemicals	613	68.3	603
						4,298		
37	Zurich Insurance Group	Switzerland	Maryland Insurance Group	100	insurance			
			Universal Underwriters Group	100	insurance	3,100E	NA	NA
			Empire Insurance Group	100	insurance			
			Zurich-American Ins Group	100	insurance	1,112	99.7	3,629
						4,212		
38	BTR Plc*	UK	BTR Dunlop Holdings	100	construction, controls	3,552	NA	2,323
			Rexnord	100	power transmission prods	533	23.9	680
						4,085		
39	Prudential Corp Plc*	UK	Jackson National Life	100	insurance	3,442	149.2	16,950
			Jackson Natl Life of Michigan	100	insurance	378	19.8	2,290
						3,820		
40	Dalgety	UK	Martin-Brower	100	food distribution	3,784	NA	NA
			Pig Improvement	100	pig breeding			
41	Daimler-Benz*	Germany	Freightliner	100	automotive	3,045	NA	NA
	AEG AG*	Germany	AEG Transportation	100	rail systems	698	NA	NA
			Other companies	100	elec equip, microelectronics			
						3,743		
42	Internationale Nederlanden	Netherlands	ING Insurance US	100	insurance	3,153	NA	NA
	Groep NV		ING Bank US	100	banking	585	NA	NA
						3,738		
43	Fujitsu Ltd*	Japan	Fujitsu (US)	100	electronics	2,024	NA	NA
			Amdahl*	45	computer systems	1,681	-588.7	1,672
						3,705		
44	Volvo AB*	Sweden	Volvo GM Heavy Truck	87	automotive	1,550	3.0	428
	VME Group NV	Netherlands	VME Americas	50	automotive	450	NA	200
	Regie Nationale des Usines Renault	France	Mack Trucks	100	automotive	1,700E	NA	NA
						3,700		
45	AEGON NV*	Netherlands	AEGON USA	100	insurance	3,563	NA	23,397
46	Petrofina*	Belgium	Fina*	86	energy	3,416	70.4	2,511
47	Roche Holding*	Switzerland	Hoffmann-La Roche	100	drugs, chemicals	2,800	NA	NA
			Genentech*	65	biotechnology	608	58.9	1,469
						3,408		
48	Anglo Amer of S Africa*	South Africa						
	De Beers Centenary	Switzerland						
	Minorco*	Luxembourg	Engelhard*	32	metals	2,151	16.7	1,279
			Terra Industries*	53	agribusiness	1,213	22.8	634
						3,364		
49	Glaxo Holdings Plc*	UK	Glaxo Inc	100	ethical pharmaceuticals	3,224	NA	NA
50	Elf Aquitaine*	France	Elf Aquitaine Inc	100	chemicals	2,557	NA	4,306
	Elf Sanofi	France	Elf Sanofi Inc	100	health & beauty products	458	NA	601
						3,015		
51	Mazda Motor Corp	Japan	AutoAlliance International	50	automotive	3,000E	NA	NA
51	Thomson SA	France	Thomson Consumer Electronics	100	consumer electronics	3,000E	NA	NA
53	Sandoz Ltd*	Switzerland	Sandoz (US)	100	drugs, chemicals	2,952	NA	NA

* Publicly traded in the U.S. in shares or ADRs. Note: Some foreign investors on the list own U.S. companies indirectly through companies in italics.
E: Estimate.   NA: Not available.

52

1993 rank	Foreign investor	Country	US investment	% owned	Industry	Revenue ($mil)	Net income ($mil)	Assets ($mil)
54	Jefferson Smurfit Group Plc	Ireland	Jefferson Smurfit Corp*	47	paper, packaging	2,948	-174.6	2,597
55	RWE*	Germany	Consol Energy	50	coal mining	1,800	-61.0	3,700
			Vista Chemical	100	chemicals	836	NA	NA
			American Nukem	100	waste management	234	NA	NA
			Heidelberg West	100	industrial machinery	71	NA	NA
						2,941		
56	Imperial Chemical Industries Plc*	UK	ICI American Holdings	100	chemicals	2,700	NA	2,400
			ICI Explosives Holdings	100	explosives	240	NA	270
						2,940		
57	Total SA*	France	Total America Inc	100	chemicals, energy	564	-37.1	1,000
	*Total Petroleum NA**	Canada	Total Petroleum Inc	100	energy	2,331	27.5	1,261
						2,895		
58	Manufacturers Life Insurance	Canada	Manufacturers Life Ins US	100	insurance	2,849	89.8	15,562
59	Fortis AMEV* Fortis AG	Netherlands Belgium	Fortis Inc	100	insurance	2,760	169.7	6,480
60	General Electric Plc*	UK	Picker International	100	medical equipment			
			AB Dick	100	office equipment	2,741	NA	NA
			Other companies	100	elec system & components			
61	Dainippon Ink & Chemicals	Japan	Sun Chemical	100	printing, chemicals	1,800E	NA	NA
			Reichhold Chemicals	100	chemicals	800E	NA	NA
			Polychrome	100	printing	120E	NA	NA
						2,720		
62	Trygg-Hansa SPP Holding	Sweden	Home Holdings*	65	insurance	2,709	-158.0	10,319
62	Saint-Gobain	France	Norton	100	ceramics, abrasives	1,383	NA	NA
			CertainTeed	100	building materials	1,326	NA	NA
						2,709		
64	Alcan Aluminium Ltd*	Canada	Alcan Aluminum Corp	100	aluminum	2,689	-57.0	1,718
65	Sun Life Assurance Co of Canada	Canada	Sun Life of Canada (US)	100	insurance	2,102	3.3	9,199
			Sun Life's US Subsidiaries	100	insurance	584	NA	4,831
						2,686		
66	Great-West Lifeco	Canada	Great-West Life Assurance	99	insurance	2,623	NA	14,629
67	Akzo Nobel NV*	Netherlands	Akzo Nobel (US)	100	chemicals, coatings	2,585	NA	2,000
68	Ferruzzi-Montedison* Group	Italy	Central Soya	100	food processing			
			Himont	100	chemicals	2,583	NA	NA
			Ausimont USA	100	chemicals			
			Other companies	100	marine equipment			
69	Michael Otto	Germany	Spiegel*	84	catalog retailing	2,532	48.7	2,211
70	General Accident Plc	UK	Gen Accident Corp of Am	100	insurance	2,531	207.0	6,704
71	Zeneca Group Plc*	UK	Zeneca Inc	100	drugs, agrochemicals	2,469	NA	2,336
72	Thomson Corp	Canada	Thomson US Holdings	100	publishing	2,468	NA	5,046
73	Canadian Pacific Ltd*	Canada	Canadian Pacific (US)	100	railroad	875	NA	3,037
	*United Dominion Inds**	Canada	United Dominion Inds (US)	100	industrial machinery	1,585	NA	914
						2,460		
74	NKK Corp*	Japan	National Steel*	76	steel	2,419	-242.4	2,304
75	Tate & Lyle*	UK	AE Staley Manufacturing	90	food distrib, processing	1,121	NA	NA
			Domino Sugar	100	sugar refining			
			PM Ag Products	100	animal feeds, molasses	1,260	NA	NA
			Other companies	100	sugar processing			
						2,381		

* Publicly traded in the U.S. in shares or ADRs. Note: Some foreign investors on the list own U.S. companies indirectly through companies in italics.
E: Estimate.   NA: Not available.

53

1993 rank	Foreign investor	Country	US investment	% owned	Industry	Revenue ($mil)	Net income ($mil)	Assets ($mil)
76	Bertelsmann AG	Germany	Bertelsmann USA	100	printing, publishing	2,357	NA	NA
77	Edmond J Safra	Switzerland						
	Saban	Switzerland	Republic New York*	28	banking	2,328	301.2	39,493
78	McDermott International*	Panama	McDermott Inc	100	heavy equipment	2,243	-26.3	2,486
79	RTZ Plc*	UK	RTZ America	100	mining	1,746	61.0	4,216
	CRA*	Australia	Comalco (US) Holding	67	aluminum	413	-5.4	324
						2,159		
80	WPP Group Plc*	UK	J Walter Thompson	100	advertising	876	NA	NA
			Ogilvy & Mather Worldwide	100	advertising	824	NA	NA
			WPP Group USA	100	marketing services	293	NA	NA
			Hill & Knowlton	100	public relations	147	NA	NA
						2,140		
81	Brascan Ltd*	Canada						
	Noranda	Canada	Noranda Aluminum	100	aluminum	1,189	NA	860
			Other companies	100	aluminum			
			Fraser	74	forest products	371	NA	229
	Trilon Financial	Canada	London Life Insurance	100	life insurance	551	NA	1,995
			Holden Group	60	financial services			
						2,111		
82	Commercial Union Plc	UK	Commercial Union Corp	100	insurance	2,089	104.5	5,651
83	Confederation Life Insurance	Canada	Confederation Life (US)	100	insurance	2,072	NA	8,178
84	Sobey Parties	Canada	Hannaford Brothers*	26	food distribution	2,055	54.6	795
85	Snecma	France	CFM International	50	aviation	2,028	2.3	1,032
86	Siebe Plc*	UK	Siebe (US)	100	controls	2,000	NA	NA
87	Royal Insurance Holdings	UK	Royal USA	100	insurance	1,988	67.1	5,325
88	J Sainsbury*	UK	Shaw's Supermarkets	100	supermarkets	1,974	NA	NA
89	George Weston	Canada	Stroehmann Bakeries	100	bakery	375		
			Interbake Foods	100	bakery	200		
			EB Eddy Paper	100	paper products	100	NA	411
			Other companies	100	canned foods	150		
	Loblaw Cos	Canada	National Tea	100	food retailing	1,050	NA	509
						1,875		
90	Mitsubishi Motors Corp	Japan	Diamond-Star Motors	100	automotive	1,850E	NA	NA
91	Broken Hill Proprietary*	Australia	BHP Petroleum (Americas)	100	energy	1,812	-37.0	1,895
			BHP Minerals	100	mining			
92	Royal Pakhoed	Netherlands	Univar*	28	chemicals	1,802	5.5	653
93	Fuji Heavy Industries*	Japan	Subaru-Isuzu Automotive	100	automotive	1,800E	NA	NA
	Isuzu Motors*	Japan						
94	National Westminster Bank Plc*	UK	National Westminster Bancorp	100	banking	1,763	298.1	23 661
95	United Biscuits (Holdings)*	UK	Keebler	100	food processing	1,733	-56 1	701
96	Bank of Tokyo Ltd*	Japan	Union Bank*	70	banking	1,266	83.1	16,391
			Bank of Tokyo Trust	100	banking	450	28.9	8,037
						1,716		
97	BOC Group Plc*	UK	BOC Inc	100	gases & health care	1,681	89.5	2,295
98	Thyssen*	Germany	Budd Co	100	auto parts	1,530	NA	NA
99	Moore Corp Ltd*	Canada	Moore Business Forms	100	business forms	1,523	NA	1,017
100	Robert Bosch GmbH	Germany	Robert Bosch Corp	100	auto parts	1,494	33.0	929

*Publicly traded in the U.S. in shares or ADRs. Note: Some foreign investors on the list own U.S. companies indirectly through companies in italics.
E: Estimate. NA: Not available.

©CTIR
University of Denver

III. POLITICS

Introduction

This activity introduces students to the dynamics of policy-making in multiethnic societies. It deals specifically with the conflict between ethnic groups competing for limited resources within a society. Students play the roles of members of ethnic groups and members of the nation's legislative body. The players must formulate their policy priorities and bargain with the other groups, eventually seeking to satisfy their goals and improve their ethnic group's position in the society. In debriefing the game, students examine and analyze the many factors that determine and influence ethnic conflict.

Objectives

Students will be able to:

- Increase their knowledge about the functions of the political process in a multiethnic society.
- Develop political bargaining skills.
- Improve comprehension of the rationale behind the nature of ethnic demands.
- Act out the processes involved in ethnic conflict situations.
- Understand what it can mean to be a member of an ethnic group in a multiethnic society.

Grade Level

7-12

Time

Two class periods

Materials

Handout #12, "Rules"
Handout #13, "Profiles"
Handout #14, "Name Tags"
Handout #15, "Demand Form"
Handout #16, "Policy Accomplishments"

Procedure

1. Display Zabros map and the initial power card distribution (Zabros 50; Abas 22; Boros 20; Obos 8) on the chalkboard or in a place where everyone can see both during the game. See Teacher Information for power card distribution and map.

2. Divide students into four groups, with the Obos having the fewest members. There should be an odd number of players in each group if possible. Distribute Handouts #12 and #13, with the appropriate profile to each player. Also distribute appropriate name tags (Handout #14).

3. Within their groups, students read over their role sheets and discuss their long range policy goals. Students decide, based on their ethnic group profiles and suggested policy options, exactly what their groups' priorities should be.

©CTIR
University of Denver

4. The Game Director reads the rules and explains the power card distribution chart.

5. Allow 5 minutes for each group to discuss general strategy and formulate its plans for bargaining with other groups. <u>At this point there should be no interaction between the groups.</u>

6. Allow 5-10 minutes for intergroup bargaining and communication. Students may communicate with other groups, with permission of that group only. Students discuss working together on policy demands and attempt to find out about the characteristics and goals of the other groups.

7. Allow 5 minutes for players to return to their groups and discuss what they learned from the other ethnic groups. <u>At this time each group must write its demand on the Demand Form (Handout #15) and submit it to the Game Director.</u>

8. Once all demand forms are received, they are read aloud by the Game Director. They should be read in the order they are received.

9. Each group may make a one-minute speech to the entire group supporting its demand.

10. Give each group 2 minutes to discuss among itself how it will vote on the demand.

11. Have each group vote, tally the vote, and redistribute power cards (if necessary). On voting, the majority rules--51 percent to pass or defeat a demand. Record results on Handout #16.

12. Play as many voting rounds as you can.

Debriefing

- Why did you vote the way you did?

- How did you feel about being a Zabro, Boro, Aba, or Obo?

- How did leaders develop in each group?

- Which ethnic group do you feel was in the best position? Why?

- If you could have been a member of any of the four groups, which one would you prefer? Why?

- Do you think the game was like the real world? Why or why not?

- What parts of the game seemed unrealistic to you? Realistic?

- How could we find out more about ethnic conflict?

- Did you find yourself feeling that your group was better than the others in any way?

- Did you begin to stereotype the other groups? Were the Obos "stupid farmers" and the Boros "dirty miners?"

Teacher Information

This game simulates the distribution of the resources of a multiethnic society through the political system. The game is organized to involve students in bargaining and decision making in a situation best described as one of ethnic conflict. Most nations of the world are comprised of two or more ethnic groups. The groups work out many different ways for distributing the resources, goods, and services of the nation. The ways that ethnic groups cope with each other through the political process are the subject of this game.

The object of the game is for students to meet as many of the goals of their ethnic group as they can. Since the goals of the various groups are not similar or complementary, a conflict situation arises when each group attempts to meet its own goals, often at the expense of other groups.

Players are members of the multiethnic society of Zabros. The game simulates the policy-making process in a multiethnic society. Students become members of four ethnic groups: Abas, Boros, Obos, and Zabros. Each of these groups has a distinct culture with its own set of values, beliefs, and behaviors which are maintained by symbols of culture. Each group has its own language, religion, and customs unique to its cultural heritage. In addition, each group maintains (or tries to maintain) its own territory.

As members of a hypothetical ethnic group, students share a common bond. This bond is composed of fundamental beliefs, issues of right and wrong, definitions of what rules should be followed, priorities, goals, and values--all of which each group sees as distinctive from those of other groups. Moreover, each group sees itself as a collective, a separate group within a larger society, i.e., Zabros. As a nation, the four groups join together only when it seems more efficient for meeting the demands of a nation. Although each group shares some characteristics with other groups (for example, a rather weak national affiliation), the groups are quite different when it comes to political aspirations. The game explores four basic ethnic political orientations. These are described in the profiles.

POWER CARD DISTRIBUTION	
Group	Power Cards
Zabros	50
Abas	22
Boros	20
Obos	8

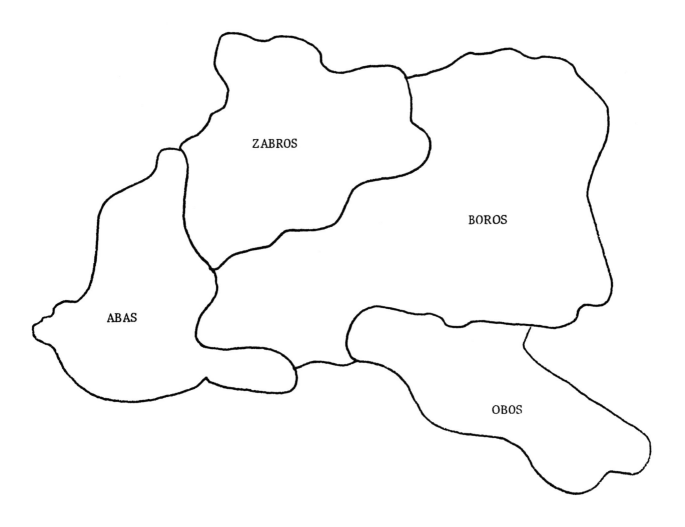

The four ethnic groups in Zabros are: 1. Zabros
2. Abas
3. Boros
4. Obos

RULES

1. Each ethnic group starts the game with a predetermined number of Zabros Power Cards. There are a total of 100 Zabros Power Cards. Each card equals 1 percent of the vote in the Zabros senate. At the beginning of the game the Zabros Power Cards are distributed as follows:

Zabros have 50 Zabros Power Cards or 50 percent of the votes in the senate. Abas have 22 Zabros Power Cards or 22 percent of the votes in the senate. Boros have 20 Zabros Power Cards or 20 percent of the votes in the senate. Obos have 8 Zabros Power Cards or 8 percent of the votes in the senate.

2. Any ethnic group can submit one demand to the assembled groups during each voting round.

3. Prior to making out a Demand Form, each group will first decide its particular strategies. Secondly, it will bargain with the other groups in an attempt to get support for its position. The game director has detailed information on how this bargaining process works.

4. To submit a demand, it must be written on a Demand Form. Before it is submitted to the Director, it must be approved by a majority of the members in your ethnic group. Each demand must state how many Zabros Power Cards the demand is worth and from what other ethnic group or groups the Zabros Power Cards are to be taken.

5. Once a demand is presented to the Game Director, it may not be changed.

6. Once the demands have been presented to the senate, each group has one minute to convince other players to vote for or against the demands. The Game Director has rules that govern how this bargaining will take place.

7. When voting, each member of an ethnic group has an equal vote (one person one vote) within that group. The majority (51 percent) decides whether that group's votes will be placed in favor of the demand or against the demand. For example, if one ethnic group of seven players has fifteen power cards and four of the players vote for a demand, the entire fifteen votes represented by the power cards would be placed in favor of the demand.

8. The senate is composed of all members of all the ethnic groups represented. All votes are decided by a majority vote of the senate. In other words, a demand that receives 51 percent of the vote in the senate would pass.

9. Each group should use its Policy Accomplishments sheets to keep track of all of the programs it has passed in the senate for its particular group.

If normal channels of bargaining and decision making do not seem to be working effectively for your group, you may resort to activities considered extraordinary and extralegal. There are two options explained below: Terrorism and Strikes.

©CTIR
University of Denver

Terrorism can be used by the two groups with the lowest amount of power cards any time after the first complete round of play. A terrorist move can only be made directly after the Demand Forms have been presented to the Game Director. Terrorism requires a majority vote of the group using the terror.

Once terror has been used, all bargaining and voting in that round stops. The terrorist may make a statement. The remaining time is used to work out a solution to the terrorist demand. All groups make an attempt to resolve the conflict. If the conflict is resolved, the group may end its terrorism. The terrorist group still must pay for this activity.

Costs: In real life, terrorism costs the society valuable human and material resources. The terrorist group must pay two power cards for using terrorism. The cards are kept out of the game for two rounds after the terrorism has ended. After two rounds, the power cards are returned to the terrorist group.

The dominant group (the group with the most power cards) must repress the terrorism if no solution can be agreed upon after one round of bargaining. For the sake of keeping order in the society, the dominant group must use its resources to prevent any terrorism. The cost to the dominant group is five power cards. The cards are kept out of the game for two rounds. Repression must be used if the terrorist group does not withdraw its terrorism by the end of the round. After the two rounds the power cards are again returned to the dominant group.

A second round of terrorism by the same group costs that group four power cards, held out for two rounds. A third round would cost six power cards. Each successive use of terrorism by the same group costs an additional two cards.

EXAMPLE OF "POWER CARD" DISTRIBUTION DURING TERRORISM			
	After one complete round	After 1st round of declared terrorism	After 2nd round of declared terrorism
Dominant group	Zabros 50	Zabros 45 (-5)*	Zabros 40 (-10)*
	Abas 22	Abas 22	Abas 22
Declares Terrorism	Boros 20	Boros 18 (-2)*	Boros 14 (1-6)*
	Obos 8	Obos 8	Obos 8
	Total = 100 Majority = 51	Total = 93 Majority = 47	Total = 84 Majority = 43
*Power cards are held out of the game for two rounds and then returned. The point loss is only temporary.			

©CTIR
University of Denver

Strikes: Each group has certain products or skills that they contribute to the economy of the Zabros nation. Any group can declare a strike at any time. The legislative process is not disrupted, the game goes on as usual. The strike will have certain costs. Each group will be penalized because they all are affected. As soon as the strike is resolved, the penalties are lifted.

Types of Strikes:

A. A food production slowdown or strike can be called by the Obos group only. The cost of an agricultural slowdown or strike per round is two power cards per group, including the Obos since they are losing money for not selling their crops. These power cards are held out of the game until the strike is resolved.

For example, if the power distribution is: Zabros--50, Abas--22, Boros--20, Obos--8 and a food strike is called by the Obos for the next round, legislation continues but the power distribution is: Zabros--48, Abas--22, Boros--18, Obos--6, for a total of 92 power cards in play. Majority needed for passing legislation is 47. For each subsequent round the strike continues, two more cards are taken from each group. Once the strike is resolved, all withheld power cards are returned to the groups.

B. A mining strike can be initiated only by the Boros. The cost of this type of strike is one power card per group. The Boros must also pay since they are out of jobs and losing money. The power cards are withheld from the game until the strike is resolved. Also, each group loses one power card for every additional round the strike continues. Legislative activity is not affected, bargaining continues. It is important that a solution to the strike is found as soon as possible to prevent a further loss of power for every group.

Note: Players should realize that terrorism and strikes are options which should be used only when all else fails. An ethnic group which proclaims terror or calls a strike prevents every group from carrying out its day-to-day affairs. This could alienate other groups, preventing them from working with the terrorizing or striking group in the future.

PROFILE-ABAS

You are Abas. The Abas are the third largest ethnic group in Zabros, according to the latest population figures. You make up 20 percent of the population. You live in a section of the country noted for its mineral wealth. However, the minerals have been depleted and no longer exist. Years ago you were a strong ethnic group with your own special language, culture, and customs. But now that your group has lost its mineral wealth, you speak the language of the Zabros (the dominate language in the country) in order to get good jobs and become more active in the government of the country.

For much of your history, your people have been workers in the mines but now there is a great need for education so that your people can hold the better "white collar" jobs that Zabros now hold. You have no universities in your region. Your group prefers to send all students to Zabros schools located in the Zabros region. You are the middle class of Zabros. Your people are satisfied, for the most part, with their jobs, families, and place in society, but you would like to be as rich as the Zabros. You are called "social ethnics." You have a limited commitment to your ethnic heritage. You participate in ethnic holidays, clubs, dances, and parades; but you would never let your ethnic practices interfere with contact or friendship with members of other ethnic groups. Specifically, your goal is to gain some of the power and you want to get better jobs and more of the government positions.

STRATEGIES

You might demand that there be the same percentage of Abas in the university as there are Zabros.

You might demand that the government provide loans so that Abas can go to college and get degrees.

You might demand that more and more government jobs be filled by Abas.

You might demand that money be invested by the government to start white collar industries, like computer firms, in your region.

You might demand that the Zabros language be taught to all people in the country as soon as possible.

You might demand that the transportation systems between the Abas region and the Zabros region be improved.

You might demand that Zabros and Abas be the only groups allowed to hold government jobs.

You might demand that only the Abas and Zabros be allowed to participate in the senate.

Remember: You can make any specific demands which reflect the goals stated in your profile.

PROFILE-BOROS

You are Boros. Your group is the largest ethnic group (in numbers) in the country, making up 40 percent of the total population. The Boros live in the central region of the country. Your region has just undergone rapid industrialization. That means that many new factories are being built and many people are moving to the cities of the region. This also means that lots of money is being invested in your region. This has been the result of the building of a seaport and a canal system linking the Boros region with the other three regions of Zabros. Your lives are changing rapidly, yet your ethnic heritage and identification are very, very important to you. You are called "ethnic nationalists." That means that you place your ethnic group ahead of the nation. You do not feel loyalty to the nation. Your loyalty rests first with your ethnic group. Religion is an important part of your ethnic heritage. In addition, .your group speaks only the Boros language. In fact, your group has made rules that restrict the use of other languages, especially Zabros, within the Boros region. If a person wants to learn the Zabros language, he or she must go to high school.

You and your people prefer to keep to yourselves, especially when marriage and friendships are concerned. Your group's strong ethnic identity combined with your improved economic conditions are leading your group in the direction of complete control over your own region from the government down to the education system. You want your own university. You want control over all education in your region. Your major goal is to gain more power in the government so that you will have more control over your own region. In fact your group feels so strongly about having local control that many people want to form their own separate nation called BOROLAND.

STRATEGIES

You might demand that all instruction in the schools of your region be in the Boros language.
You might demand universities in the Boros region be equal to those in the Zabros region.
You might demand to have schools that will train adults and workers.
You might demand that the government support the development of industry in your region by backing all loans.
You might demand that the Boros have complete control over their industries and that includes prices.
You might demand that the Boros people have their own radio, T.V., and newspapers.
You might demand that your group be given a bigger vote in the senate.
You might demand that your ethnic holidays become national holidays.

Remember: You can make any specific demands which reflect the goals stated in your profile.

PROFILE-OBOS

You are Obos. Your group makes up 25 percent of the population of Zabros. You live in the poorest section of the country. Most of you are rural farmers and make your living by growing wheat and vegetables. You are considered by the other ethnic groups to be the lower class of the nation. Without the aid of the government through welfare programs and aid to farmers, many of your people would die. Therefore, your people are loyal to the government because they must be, not because they want to be.

You are called "communal ethnics." Your community's practices and beliefs are based on ethnic customs and practices. There is no difference between community life and ethnic life. You feel a very strong attachment to each other and prefer to be with other Obos. You are willing to associate with other ethnic groups only when necessary to get something you need. Your group is not interested at the present time in the government or the nation except when programs that will benefit Obos are considered.

Because of the changes in Boros, which is next to Obos, many of your people are working in Boros and are beginning to think like the Boros. Therefore, many of you are becoming convinced that Boros and Obos should be self- governing and not controlled by the national government. There is no university in Obos; it is the most poorly educated region of the nation. Twenty-five percent of your people cannot read or write and the government at the present time does not provide aid for education. Your goal is to maintain government aid programs. In fact, you want government aid for education and you want the government to make sure your people are never hungry. You practice a religion that is not recognized by the government and you want it recognized.

STRATEGIES

You might demand technical and vocational schools for your region. You might demand a
  university, but not until you have the other schools.
You might demand that the government give you a radio station for Obos operated by Obos.
You might demand that: (1) your language be protected, and (2) the government guarantee
  that people speaking the language will not be denied jobs.
You might demand that the government start programs that will provide fertilizer and seed
  for all farmers in the region.
You might demand that prices be set on food which will assure the farmer he will make
  money on his crops.
You might demand money from the government to support ethnic heritage programs and
  events.

Remember: You can make any specific demands which reflect the goals stated in your profile.

PROFILE-ZABROS

You are Zabros. The country of Zabros gets its name from your ethnic group. You are the major group responsible for the unification of the four regions of the country into one nation. The nation's capital city is in the Zabros region, as well as most of the government offices and jobs. The only two universities in the country are in the Zabros region. Your language is the official language of the nation and must be spoken by applicants to get a government job. Your region does not contain heavy industry like steel, but it is the home of many "white collar" businesses such as computer firms and research firms. Your group controls the government and you feel things should stay that way. Your group only makes up 10 percent of the population, but your group makes more money than anyone in the three other ethnic groups. You are called "state nationalists." This means that your loyalties are more toward the nation and government and less toward the ethnic group to which you belong. Your ethnic customs are not important. What is important is the protection of the nation and the government in which you are the most powerful group. Your goal is to maintain control of the government and to control what other groups can and cannot do. You might give up some power to keep the other groups happy, but you do not want to lose control of the government.

STRATEGIES

You might demand that each region have a university, but insist that your language be the only language spoken in these schools.

You might demand that each region have a university as long as your region has two more universities than the others.

You might demand that the senate can never allow other regions to have radio, television, or newspapers unless the Zabros agree.

You might demand that no demands be passed in the senate without Zabros approval.

You might demand that all government offices be filled by Zabros only.

You might demand that money be spent to increase cultural and ethnic holidays in the regions, but only Zabros holidays are national holidays.

You might demand that the government furnish aid to the Obos if they let the Zabros set food prices.

Remember: You can make any specific demands which reflect the goals stated in your profile. You will fight all possible attempts to take away your control of the government.

ZABROS	**ZABROS**
ABAS	**ABAS**
BOROS	**BOROS**
OBOS	**OBOS**

DEMAND FORM

WE THE_____ DEMAND_____

_____

_____

_____

THIS DEMAND IS WORTH_____ ZABROS POWER CARDS.

THESE CARDS WILL COME FROM THE_____

- -

WE THE_____ DEMAND_____

_____

_____

_____

THIS DEMAND IS WORTH_____ ZABROS POWER CARDS.

THESE CARDS WILL COME FROM THE_____

©CTIR
University of Denver

POLICY ACCOMPLISHMENTS

Policy Demand Make	Failed	Passed	Supporters

Introduction

Making decisions in real life situations often seems very difficult because of complex factors and emotions which complicate the situation. Nevertheless, as society increasingly becomes faced with more complex situations, the effective citizen must make difficult decisions. How well the students make such decisions in the future may depend, in part, on their understanding of past situations as well as cause and effect relationships. They also should understand how emotional feelings and insufficient information can result in undesirable consequences.

The object of Self-Defense is to demonstrate to students how countries, acting in what they consider to be their own self-interests, may aggravate or create a situation which they really do not want to happen. The situation parallels that of Europe in 1914. It may be used to introduce the outbreak of World War I, the causes of war, or the problems and consequences of decision making. The students should not be told the simulation is of World War I until the activity is completed.

This is a fairly tightly controlled simulation, but the teacher, acting as Control, should exercise additional control if necessary. This may be done by issuing news bulletins or serving as advisor to the individual countries.

When introducing the game, stress to students that they are in decision-making capacities for their respective governments and must think as patriotic persons for their governments. Do not allow them to ignore vital information given to them.

Objectives

Students will be able to:

- Make decisions in an historically simulated situation.
- Gain a first-hand view of cause and effect relationships.
- Realize that inadequate information and emotionalism can result in disastrous decisions and undesirable consequences.
- Introduce World War I and some causes of its outbreak.
- Examine the threat that the emotional aspect of nationalism has had and can have for the future.

Grade Level   6-12

Time   Two class periods

Written by Bethene Bowlby Sears

Materials

Handout #17, "Background Information"
Handout #18, "Symbols and Badges"
Handout #19, "Map"
Handout #20, "Assassination Story"
Handout #21, "Top Secret Messages"
Handout #22, "Key"
Handout #23, "Common Results"

Procedure

1. Prepare Top Secret Information packets (Handouts #17-#19). Color country symbols and badges in suggested colors. Cut symbols out and glue them on folders with tabs. Write "Top Secret Information" on the tabs. Cut out badges and enclose straight pins (one badge for the diplomat and one badge for the alternate). In each folder place two badges, the background information, and a map.

2. Divide the class into the governments of five countries. Stress the basic rules:

You are patriotic and must act in what seems at that point to be in the best interests of your country based on the information you have. You may not ignore vital considerations or change preset policies (as stated in the background information).

Each country should select one diplomat and one alternate. These are the only ones who may move to talk with other countries and only when carrying definite official messages and when wearing official badges.

No spying on top secret information is allowed.

All diplomats and alternates must report to Control before and after going to another country. They are to tell Control any decisions they have made. No country is allowed to tell another country its decision on any matter before that country tells Control. For example, if a diplomat from Country A asks Country B to support them, Country B will say, "We will discuss your proposition and our diplomat will get back to you."

3. Pass out the information packets for the respective countries. Tell students to study the information and the maps thoroughly. They should then select their diplomats and display their national symbols.

4. Distribute Handout #20 to all countries. Allow each country to read and discuss.

5. Give Nurdian Empire II (Handout #21) to the Nurdian Empire. The Nurdian diplomat will then report to Control and reveal its decision. Since this is a very controlled simulation, the Nurdian decisions should correspond to Grainland II. If not, Control will have to supply

71

©CTIR
University of Denver

the handout. The Nurdian diplomat will then proceed to Grainland. After the Nurdian diplomat returns to the Nurdian Empire, Control will call the Grainland diplomat to come and get Grainland II. Grainland usually supports the Nurdian Empire. If so, give the Nurdian diplomat Nurdian Empire III.

6. The Nurdian diplomat will now come to Control with the message it is going to send to Southland. When the Nurdian diplomat returns to Nurdian Empire, call the diplomat from Southland and deliver Southland II. The diplomat from Southland will now come with its message to Northland. After the Southland diplomat returns home, call the Northland diplomat and deliver Northland II. The Northland diplomat reports the decision to Control. Call the Southland diplomat to Control and deliver Southland III. Call the Swangola diplomat to Control and deliver Swangola II. Record Swangola's decision.

7. Call the Grainland diplomat and deliver Grainland III. Have the diplomat report the decision to Control and record.

8. Distribute Grainland III to Grainland and All Countries I to all countries except Grainland. Have all countries report their decisions to Control.

9. Compile all data. If the simulation goes as it usually does, Control will announce a state of war and which countries are involved. Distribute Handouts #22 and #23 along with the notes taken during the simulation.

Debriefing

- Which country was technically responsible for the outbreak of war during the game?

- Which country was morally responsible?

- Could this war have been avoided? How?

- Compare the game to the outbreak of World War I and discuss.

Follow-up

Brainstorm concepts that helped to bring about World War I that still exist today. Discuss possible solutions for today and the future.

BACKGROUND INFORMATION

TOP SECRET--Nurdian Empire

Empire suffers from a number of internal problems. The government is that of a dual monarchy: one Nurd and one Dian Emperor, who are supposed to have equal powers. However, Dians are becoming increasingly discontent, for regardless of what should be, it is apparent that power and control rests with the aging Fred Nurd, the Nurd Emperor. The Dian monarchy might as well be nonexistent.

Further, the heir to the throne is Frank Nurd, who is so stupid that everyone is concerned for the destiny of the Empire when Fred Nurd dies. Frank is given "figurehead" errands to run in order to keep him out of the way.

In order to distract attention from domestic problems, the Nurdian Empire has a policy of expanding the Empire into the South Sea region. Since Northland would also like to gain control of this area, Northland and the Nurdian Empire are not on good terms. However, your Empire recently gained practical control over two Southland Provinces, Ouida and Hangolia, which you expect to formally annex soon.

The Nurdian Empire is allied with Grainland (which is very strong militarily) and Telico in a defensive pact. This provides that if any of the three countries is attacked, the other two members of the alliance will come to her aid to help her preserve her sovereignty. The treaty makes no provision for coming to the aid of a member of the alliance who initiates aggression.

TOP SECRET--Grainland

Grainland lies between two traditionally powerful enemies, Swangola and Northland (see map). Swangola, in particular, is bitter from her defeat in the Swan-Grain War. To guard against possible future aggression on the part of either Swangola or Northland, your government has taken several precautionary measures. Among these are:

1. A defensive alliance with the Nurdian Empire and Telico. This alliance is solely a defense pact. The agreement is that if any one of the three countries in the alliance is aggressed upon by any outside power the other two countries will help the attacked nation preserve its sovereignty. The treaty makes no provision for coming to the aid of a member of the alliance who initiates aggression.

2. A detailed and thorough arms buildup. The arms buildup has been developed in order to guarantee the integrity of the country and to discourage attack by either Swangola or Northland.

3. A detailed mobilization plan for the armed forces. This has been drawn up in detail in advance in order to give your country the best possible chance to defend itself in the event of aggression against you.

After the Swan-Grain War, Swangola, suffering from defeat and from a phobia about Grainland, sought some sort of alliance, and has probably made one of some sort with your enemy Northland. Should this be an aggressive alliance, this would create a situation whereby you could be attacked by two major powers from both sides (a two-front war).

To preserve the integrity of your country, the only hope in such an eventuality is to prevent invasion from either front. This means that if it becomes apparent that they are likely to attack, Grainland must strike first in order to prevent total collapse. Hesitation will spell doom militarily. As a result, after you have designed a total mobilization plan for your troops and material is given, all troops and materials will have priority on all roads and will move out in all directions toward your borders.

To the South, some troops will cross into your allied country of the Nurdian Empire, for they are weak militarily and may not repel an invasion by a foreign power who might decide to invade through them.

On the Northland front, troops will move to the vicinity of the border and merely stage a holding action until the Swangolese front is eliminated. Then Northland may be defeated at leisure, as the balance of troops return from the Swangolese front.

The Swangolese front is the most threatening. In order to prevent total disaster, Swangola must be knocked out of the war immediately, which will eliminate the most threatening of the vice-like, two-front situation. To do this, Swangola must be invaded swiftly and by surprise. Because of terrain and previous invasion, the only feasible route is through Ludland. This means risking antagonizing Insuland, who has declared that she will ensure Grainland's defeat. Swangola must be defeated quickly before she can invade Grainland.

TOP SECRET--Northland

Although a very large country, Northland is a very backward nation politically, militarily, diplomatically, economically, and in its transportation and communication networks. The people are becoming increasingly discontent. For several years, there has been a succession of small revolts as well as growing organizations of a political and economic nature which oppose the existing system.

Your government, aware of the general backwardness of your country compared to other powers, conducted a secret investigation to determine the degree of the various problems. This secret report indicated to you (last year) that should Northland become involved in ANY war against ANY major power in the next five years, you will suffer total and utter defeat. The conclusion was that war must be avoided for at least that amount of time. Luckily, no foreign power is aware of this report.

Your economic advisors have informed you that one of the major factors causing economic retardation is the lack of access to a warm-water seaport. A previous attempt to gain one by aggression failed. Therefore, Northland has adopted a policy by which you hope to gain the favor of similar peoples in the South Sea region in order to acquire access to such a port. Consequently, your ministry of propaganda has been attempting to create a friendly, "big brother" protector role for Northland among the similar peoples in the South Sea region. This policy has created some ill will toward Northland on the part of the Nurdian Empire, which has been seeking control over the South Sea region itself.

Northland has a defensive alliance with Swangola and Insuland. Under the terms of this alliance, if an outside power aggresses against any of the members, the other two allies have pledged all military assistance necessary for the preservation of the, attacked country's sovereignty. Northland views the two most likely countries that might aggress against her to be the Nurdian Empire and Grainland, which is a powerful traditional enemy.

TOP SECRET--Southland

Southland is a comparatively small and powerless country, but a very proud one. Although the ethnic heritage of the country's population is mixed, many people are considered similar to those living in Northland.

Recently, Southland has been severely threatened by a comparatively powerful northern neighbor, the Nurdian Empire. The Empire has, by various means, been snatching provinces of Southland and bringing them into the Nurdian Empire. Recently, for example, they have gained practical control of two more provinces, Ouida and Hangolia, forcing your comparatively weak and defenseless government into granting them formal control soon.

A declaration of war by Southland against them would only be, practically speaking, an invitation for them to invade and take your entire country. The inability of your government to prevent the nibbling aggression has caused a number of secret patriotic groups to form to fight, by various means, for the integrity of their country or provinces.

Apparently Southland's "ace in the hole" is Northland, which has been stating that, as a major power, she intends to protect and cooperate with all similar peoples to stop aggression against any such similar peoples anywhere by any other powers.

TOP SECRET--Swangola

Swangola is one of the major powers shown on the map. The principal threat to Swangolese security is Grainland, a traditional enemy who defeated you in the Swan-Grain War. As such, Grainland, who has armed herself "to the teeth," is a serious threat to the sovereignty of your country.

In order to preserve as much security as possible, you have a defensive alliance with Insuland and Northland. This alliance provides that if any of the members are attacked by a nonmember country, the other two countries will come to the aid of the one aggressed upon. It is the hope of Swangola that this defense pact, joined by three apparently strong countries located strategically around Grainland, will help save Swangola from Grainland's aggression.

SYMBOLS AND BADGES

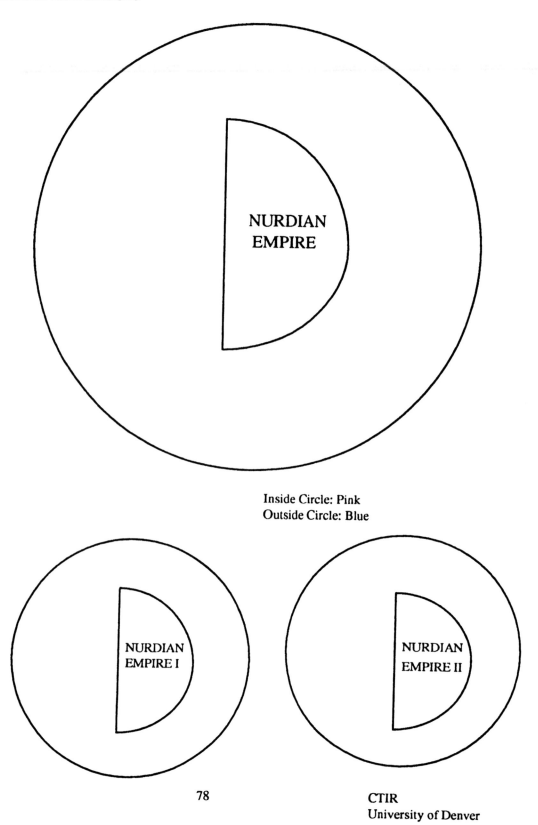

Inside Circle: Pink
Outside Circle: Blue

78

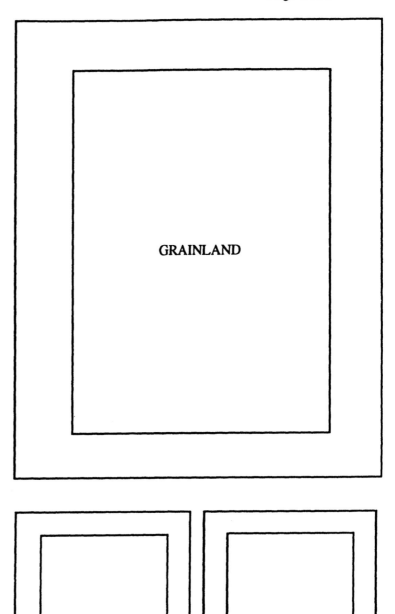

Inside Square: White

Outside Square: Green

CTIR
University of Denver

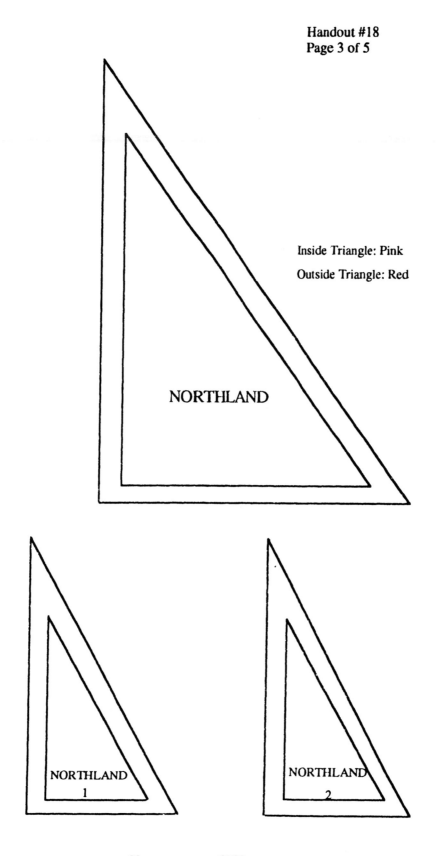

Inside Triangle: Pink

Outside Triangle: Red

NORTHLAND

NORTHLAND
1

NORTHLAND
2

CTIR
University of Denver

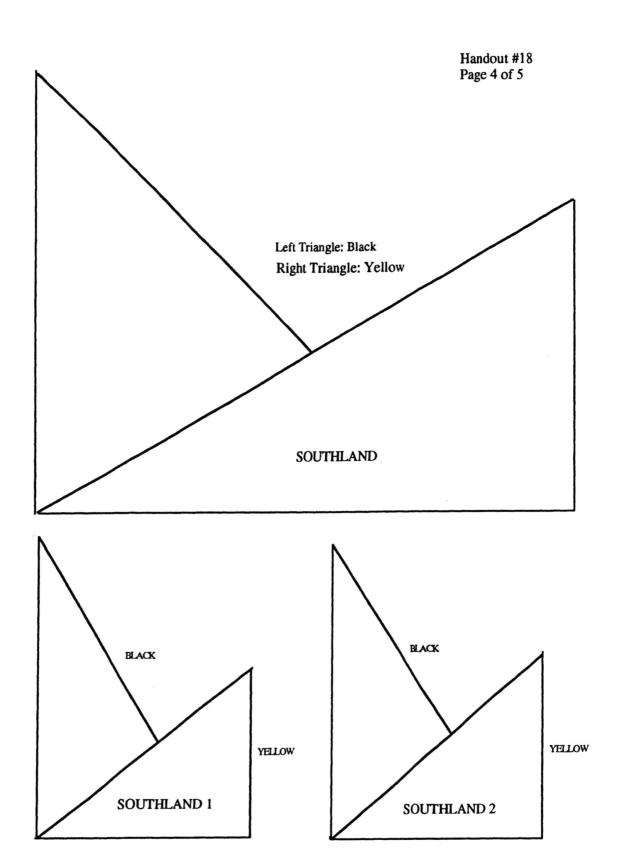

Left Triangle: Black
Right Triangle: Yellow

SOUTHLAND

BLACK

YELLOW

SOUTHLAND 1

BLACK

YELLOW

SOUTHLAND 2

CTIR
University of Denver

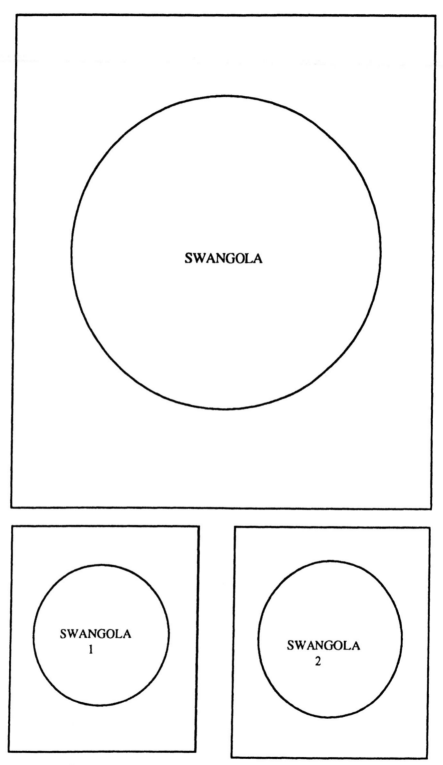

Rectangle: Orange
Circle: Yellow

CTIR
University of Denver

MAP

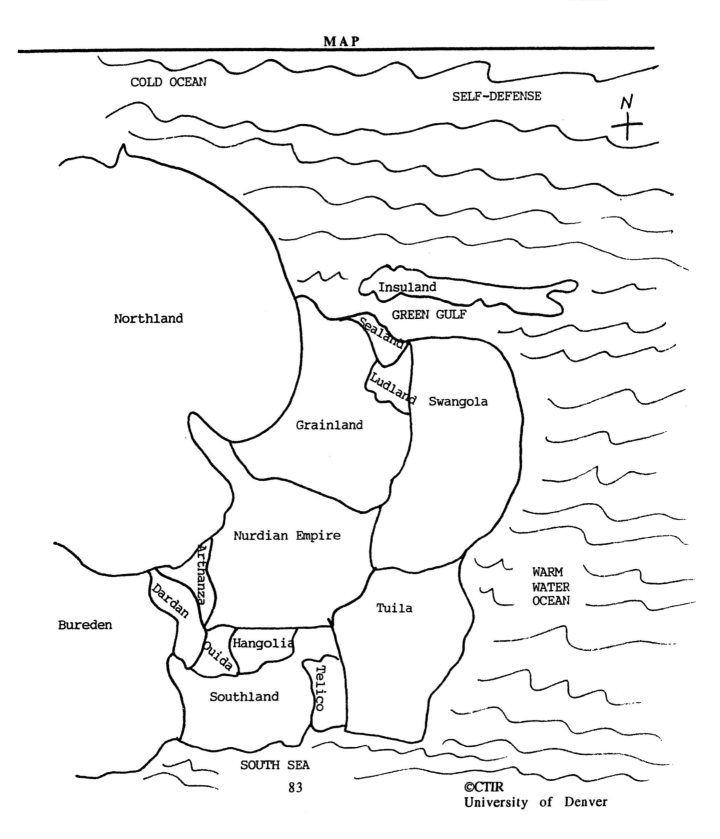

COLD OCEAN

SELF-DEFENSE

N

Insuland

GREEN GULF

Sealand

Northland

Ludland

Swangola

Grainland

Nurdian Empire

WARM
WATER
OCEAN

Arthanza

Dardan

Tuila

Bureden

Ouida

Hangolia

Telico

Southland

SOUTH SEA

83

ASSASSINATION STORY

The Nurdian Empire recently gained practical control over the two provinces of Oida and Hangolia, which used to be part of Southland.

The heir to the throne of the Nurdian Empire is Frank Nurd, a rather unintelligent man. Frank Nurd was sent to the provinces to represent the Nurdian Empire in the proceedings to officially transfer control of the provinces from Southland to the Nurdian Empire.

Mrs. Frank Nurd, a rather superstitious woman, was told by her tealeaf reader that disaster would befall them if she traveled with her husband to the ceremonies. Consequently, she elected to travel separately to the site and meet Frank there.

The inability of the government of Southland to stop the nibbling aggression of the Nurdian Empire has resulted in several secret patriotic groups which use various means, including terrorism and assassination, to fight for the integrity of their country or provinces.

The government of Southland, aware of rumors of a possible assassination attempt on Frank Nurd, stepped up security for the event, informed the Nurdian government of its knowledge, and invited them to increase their own security guard. The Nurdian Empire sent no reply.

The patriotic group planning the assassination, the Black Arms, became aware of increased security measures. As a result, the Black Arms planted several assassins along the route it was announced that Frank Nurd would take to the building where the ceremonies were to take place.

The Frank Nurd procession followed the announced route. Several assassins fired at him, but missed. Several others decided not to fire. As the Nurds were uninjured, they continued and performed their duties at the ceremony.

While the ceremony was taking place, security guards decided that exiting the city by the same announced route might be dangerous. So, the plan was made to pretend to take the announced route, but to turn right quickly at the first intersection. After the ceremonies, the procession left the city according to the revised plan, except for one vehicle. That vehicle happened to be the one in which Frank Nurd was riding. It followed the original, announced route alone.

The assassins tried again. This time, one succeeded. The driver of the Nurd vehicle maintained afterward that no one told him of the changed exit route.

TOP SECRET--Nurdian Empire II

The heir to the throne of the Nurdian Empire has been assassinated by Southland nationalists. Which policy to you wish to adopt?

A. Ignore the situation and be glad to be rid of the idiot.
B. Demand a formal apology and punishment of the assassins, then forget it and be glad.
C. Insist that the Southland government meet an ultimatum of certain demands.

Notes:

1. Both options A and B will make the Nurdian Empire appear weak and thereby vulnerable to further disruptive actions or assassinations by patriotic, but terroristic, groups of "pipsqueak" South Sea countries over which your Empire is attempting to gain control.

2. Option C gives Frank Nurd a chance to serve his country just one time, even though dead. Expansion plans for the Empire have earmarked Southland as the next area to be annexed. By listing demands (which would mean, in essence, the subjugation of Southland to control by your Empire), such as an apology and indemnity, one of two things should happen:

   a. Southland will agree to them and you have achieved your objective easily.

   b. She will refuse, which will put you in the light of a "wronged" nation. You might then regard the Southland government's refusal as approval of the assassination, which would make Southland an aggressor. This would give you an excuse to attack, and you could easily conquer her militarily.

The main difficulty with Option C is international opinion regarding who is the aggressor nation. Maybe another country would agree to side with your point of view--perhaps your ally, Grainland?

DECISION TIME: A, B, or C?

DELIVER MESSAGE(S)

©CTIR
University of Denver

TOP SECRET--Grainland II

You have been asked by your ally, the Nurdian Empire, to support her in the view that the assassination of Frank Nurd is an act of aggression against the Nurdian Empire. Will you agree to that?

POINTS TO CONSIDER:

You are aware of and approve of the Nurdian Empire's policy to expand into the weak South Sea region. Such control might make possible your own "Drive to the West," which includes constructing a railway link to the rich oil fields of Bureden. Obviously, the Nurdian Empire is using the assassination incident to further her expansion.

DECISION TIME: Yes or No?

SEND MESSAGE

- -

TOP SECRET--Nurdian Empire III

You have received a message from Grainland saying that she will support you.

SEND MESSAGE TO SOUTHLAND

TOP SECRET--Southland II

The Nurdian Empire has presented you with a list of demands which, if met, means that you will be virtually under the control of that Empire. You have a decision to make.

OPTIONS:

A. Agree to the demands, humble yourself, and allow your country to become a puppet of the aggressive Empire.

B. Refuse the demands and prepare to fight honorably for the sovereignty of your country, even though you know you will lose.

C. Refuse the demands and seek help from some friendly power--Northland?

DECISION TIME: A, B, or C?

SEND MESSAGES

- -- -

TOP SECRET--Northland II

Southland, not wishing to accede to the conditions of an ultimatum given to her by the Nurdian Empire, which if met, would mean giving the Empire power to rule Southland, has sent a message to you for help. In the message, she reminded you of your policy to protect similar peoples. You must reply.

OPTIONS:

A. Fearing war, tell her you will not support her, thereby losing face, the benefits of the similar people policy, and the possibility of a warm-water seaport which you need.

B. Save face, the policy of similar people, and the hope of a warm water port by telling her you will back her. Then make a show of support by placing some troops near the Nurdian border, being careful to keep them inside Northland's territory.

NOTE: Plan B can avoid war and hopefully cause the Nurdian Empire to back down, as she is comparatively weak and does not know just how weak Northland is.

MAKE DECISION, SEND MESSAGE, AND TAKE ACTION

TOP SECRET--Southland III

Northland will support you. It is mobilizing troops along the Northland- Nurdian border.

- -

TOP SECRET--Swangola II

Since the assassination, the situation has been very tense. Northland has amassed troops on the Nurdian and Grainland borders. The Nurdian Empire has troops near the Southland border. In such a tense situation, only one match is needed to ignite a war. It is important to protect Swangola from possible enemies. You need to make a decision.

OPTIONS:

A. Do nothing except wait and see.

B. Proclaim neutrality now, disavowing all alliances with any country in the area.

C. Send troops to reinforce border defenses near Grainland in case war breaks out and Grainland decides to attack you.

DECISION: A, B, or C?

- -

TOP SECRET--Grainland III

Your enemies, Swangola and Northland, have both amassed troops near your borders. Northland is known to be friendly with Southland, who is the enemy of your ally, the Nurdian Empire. You have a decision to make:

A. Wait and see, at the risk of being invaded.

B. Mobilize now, before invasion spells defeat.

DECISION: A or B?

TOP SECRET--All Countries (except Grainland)

EMERGENCY! Grainland has mobilized. Grainland has the mightiest military machine of all the countries on the map. If she attacks you, you will most likely lose a war to her. Her powerful troops and unbelievably strong military machine are rapidly approaching all of her borders.

Perhaps you may want to decide to explain to Grainland any previous actions you may have taken that might have offended her.

Or, you may want to simply plead for peace and try to settle the situation without involving armed might.

In any event, if you decide to act, you must act NOW, before it is too late.

- -

TOP SECRET--Grainland IV

To stop mobilization now will throw your armed forces into total chaos and confusion which would take a MINIMUM of two weeks to straighten out, leaving your country entirely defenseless for that period of time. You need to make a decision.

OPTIONS:

A. Halt mobilization, trust Swangola and Northland, and be entirely defenseless for at least two weeks.

B. Allow mobilization to continue as planned.

DECISION: A or B?

KEY

Countries:

Grainland	Germany
Nurdian Empire	Austro-Hungarian Empire
Telico	Italy
Northland	Russia
Swangola	France
Southland	Serbia
Insuland	Great Britain
Ludland	Belgium
Ouida and Hangolia	Bosnia and Herzegovina
South Sea region	The Balkans

Background information given for the countries is true.

Alliances:

Grainland/Nurdian Empire/Telico	Triple Alliance
Northland/Swangola/Insuland	Triple Entente

Wars:

Swan-Grain War	Franco-Prussian War
Previous attempt by Northland to gain a warm-water port	Russo-Japanese War

Policies:

Grainland's "Drive to the West"	Germany's "Drive to the East"
Northland's policy of similar peoples	Pan-Slavism

The Assassination:

Frank Nurd	Archduke Franz Ferdinand
Black Arms	Black Hand

The assassination took place June 28, 1914, at Sarajevo, Bosnia. The assassination story is true, with substituted names.

90

KEY

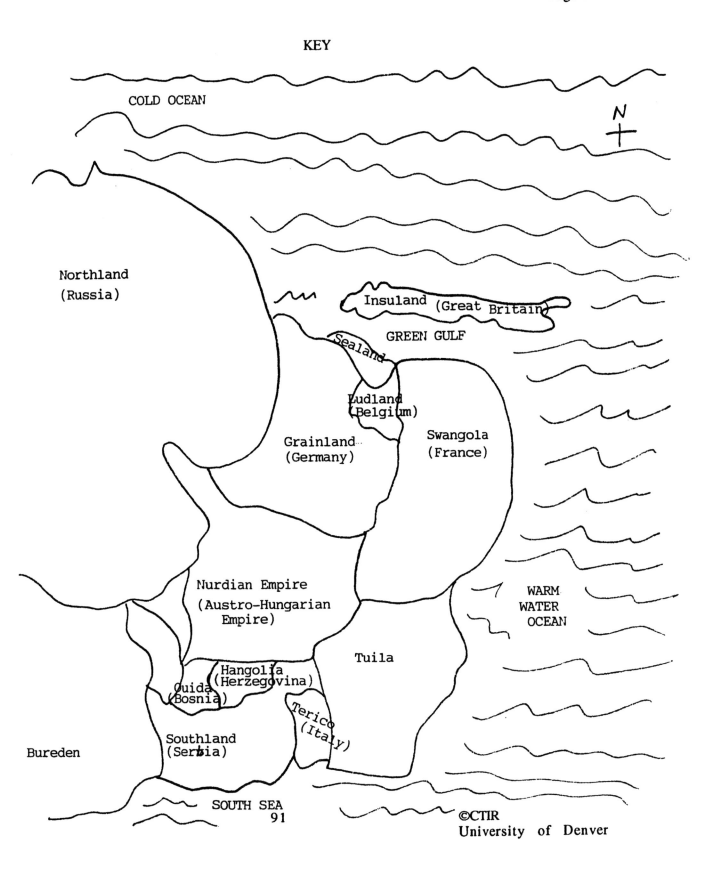

COLD OCEAN

N

Northland
(Russia)

Insuland (Great Britain)

Sealand

GREEN GULF

Ludland
(Belgium)

Grainland
(Germany)

Swangola
(France)

Nurdian Empire
(Austro-Hungarian
Empire)

WARM
WATER
OCEAN

Tuila

Hangolia
(Herzegovina)

Ouida
(Bosnia)

Terico
(Italy)

Bureden

Southland
(Serbia)

SOUTH SEA
91

COMMON RESULTS

By mistake, Northland, uncoordinated as usual, massed troops near Grainland as well as the Nurdian Empire.

Grainland troops invaded both Northland and Swangola. They entered Swangola through Ludland.

Both because of its promise to protect Ludland and because of its secret defensive pact with Swangola and Northland, Insuland declared war on Grainland.

Swangola and Northland answered Grainland's attack with declarations of war on her.

The Nurdian Empire and Telico responded to Insuland's declaration of war on Grainland by declaring war on her, since she was aggressing against Grainland.

Then, because of the secret, defensive alliances, war existed between Insuland/ Northland/Swangola versus Grainland/Nurdian Empire/Telico. Southland, of course, joined Insuland, Northland, and Swangola.

CREATING A POLITICAL PLATFORM

Introduction

When a candidate runs for political office such as president or legislative representative, his/her party generally summarizes its positions on important issues in a statement known as the party platform. The policy statements in the party platform are the result of compromises among the different groups or factions that make up the party. Each candidate will address the major issues in the party platform during the campaign so the voters will know where the candidate stands on the important issues.

The issues in a campaign affect many different groups of voters, including farmers, ranchers, businessmen, consumers, the elderly, the poor, trade and labor unions, environmentalists, miners, factory workers, oil workers, truck drivers, etc. The party platform must include concessions to these various groups in order to produce a coalition of voters sufficient to elect the candidate.

This activity is recommended as a culminating activity for a unit on politics, government, even energy. This activity is most effective after the students have been studying important issues in the country or community.

Objectives

Students will be able to:

• Analyze the issues in a campaign.
• Increase their awareness of the various sides of important issues.

Grade Level

6-12

Time

Two to three class periods

Materials

Construction or poster paper
Magic markers
Safety pins
Masking tape

Procedure

1. Begin the activity by dividing the students into groups of six or eight. Tell the groups that they will be representing a particular political party in an upcoming election. Instruct each group to select a party name, a party slogan and a candidate for the election. The candidate should be selected in accordance with an actual election taking place in the community or country; i.e. if there is a mayoral or presidential race taking place, the various parties should select a candidate for mayor or president, respectively.

2. Create a ballot containing the names of each of the candidates and their respective parties for the election to be held the next day.

3. Allow students approximately thirty minutes to design and create their posters and buttons utilizing available materials.

4. Have each student in each group represent a particular interest group, such as labor, miners, truckers, etc. The interest groups can be selected from the list in the introduction, or the students can develop a list from their own knowledge of the local groups who might be involved in the upcoming election.

5. Inform each party that they must now draft a party platform which should include a statement or position on each of the major issues one might see in an election (e.g., energy, jobs, economics, the environment, crime, etc.). If the class is studying a particular issues, such as energy, or if the election actually occurring in the community focuses on a particular issue, you should have each party focus their attention and resulting platform on that issues. The platform should be designed to appeal to as many of the groups of voters as possible. Each group should strive to develop a platform that will actually enable their particular candidate to win the election, and not simply a platform that appeals to win the election, and not simply a platform that appeals to each of the various interest groups.

6. Allow the groups thirty minutes to develop and write their party platforms on a second sheet of poster paper.

7. Tell the candidates in each group that they will each be allowed five minutes the following day to make a speech to the remainder of the class. Tell the candidates to be sure their speech serves two purposes: 1) presents the party platform to the voters; and 2) seeks to persuade the voters that they should vote for this particular candidate.

8. Begin class on the second day by allowing the party groups to meet and review the speech prepared by the party's candidate.

9. Allow each group five minutes to deliver its campaign speech. During the speech, the other members of the party can display the previously-designed campaign posters, slogans and buttons.

10. After each group has delivered its speech, hold an election. Provide each students with a ballot and allow them a few minutes to vote. Count the votes as soon as possible and declare the results to the class.

Debriefing

• How did your party decide upon its particular platform? Did an interest group within the party persuade the party to adopt a chosen platform on an issue? which group? Which issues?

• Did your final platform represent a compromise positions? Which interest group compromised the most? The least?

• Did your final platform satisfy everyone in your party?

94

- How did your party select the party candidate? Did you focus on electability? Popularity? Strength of convictions? Other?

- How does this exercise differ from "real" politics?

Introduction

A significant percentage of the leaders in the United States during the 1980s called for building up defensive strength to the point that no other nation in the world was going to dare challenge the U.S. anytime or anywhere. This necessitated an increase each year of the Department of Defense budget.

This increase in military spending had an obvious and dramatic impact on promises to cut budgets and deal with inflation. Increased military expenditures also forced cutbacks in social programs (e.g., health, education, welfare, transportation, etc.) in order to meet the budget.

Students in this activity are assigned the task of writing their own decision-making simulation on the issue of government spending for military or social programs.

Objectives

Students will be able to:

• Develop an awareness of the tradeoffs involved in deciding how public funds are spent.
• Recognize the complexity of the arms issue.
• Introduce basic research techniques and resource materials appropriate to the missiles versus meals issue.
• Develop a classroom simulation activity which explores the decision to spend money on guns or butter.

Grade Level

9-12

Time

One to two weeks

Materials

Handout #24, "Outline"

Procedure

1. Divide the class into groups of four students. Explain to the students that they are going to develop a simulation activity around the decision to spend more money on military programs (e.g., weapons, or missiles) or social programs (e.g., education, health care). This is a crucial issue facing many countries in our world today.

2. Review the information presented in the Introduction, outlining the future plans for military spending and the potential impact on social programs specifically and the economy in general.

3. Have each group research the current debate between those who advocate increasing military spending and those who favor maintaining or increasing funding for social programs. Students should be encouraged to use all the data they collect in their

©CTIR
University of Denver

simulation game. Current newspapers, periodicals, and journals in specialized areas such as arms and disarmament, defense policy, and international affairs should provide useful information.

4. Distribute Handout #24. Review and discuss the procedure with each of the groups.

5. Using all the information collected, have students develop a simulation which focuses on the debate to increase military or social programs spending.

6. Allow time for each group to present its simulation to the class. As a class, students should evaluate each simulation and help each group iron out any problems. It might be a good idea to identify the top three simulations and have the entire class work on improving them.

7. The most important part of any simulation activity is the debriefing. Students should develop a set of good questions that encourage discussion about the real world situations their game is simulating. Remind students that a game is a simulation of reality, in this particular case the debate over whether to spend public funds on military programs or social programs. Students should be encouraged to relate their simulations of reality to more complex issues in the real world.

Follow-up   Substitute building more prisons for military spending and have students develop simulations. Continue activity as described above.

OUTLINE

In designing your own simulation, follow each of the following steps. A good game has at least these six elements, but that does not mean it cannot include more.

1. Identify your objectives or the purpose of the game. What part of reality, what real world issue are you trying to simulate? For example, set up a role play activity where the pros and cons of various expenditures are debated in Congress/Parliament.

    a. Dramatize some part of reality, e.g., you can simulate the bargaining process between legislators for social programs and those in favor of increasing military spending.

    b. Teach a concept, e.g., trade-offs, conflict/conflict resolution, change, or compromise.

    c. Give people a feeling for another culture of an upcoming new experience, e.g., role-playing activities which focus on doing something your class has never done before-- experiencing another culture, debating an issue, deciding on national priorities.

2. Develop a model or detailed outline of the process you have chosen to best serve your objectives. You might begin your game with a story scenario, a film, or even a true description of an event or a particular issue facing a society. This will set the stage for what you plan to do in the simulation.

3. Identification of actors or teams in your simulation. What roles do individuals play? How many teams? Do students interact as themselves, as members of a government, or do they represent lobby groups or even countries?

4. Clearly state what is the activity in the game. What do participants do? How do participants interact? What are the means of exchange or interchange between participants? Do they trade for money, power, or control of a country? Are there any specific resources to be used for trading or for competition?

5. What are the rules or procedures for interchange, competition, or trade? Be precise about how participants interact and what rules govern their interaction behavior. You should carefully define any special procedures, penalties, or prizes that might result from certain actions.

6. Make sure you have a general set of understandable rules which define the parameters of the game. Time, number of players, and permissible behavior should be included.

Writing your own simulation is not that difficult. Think of all the board games you have played. Many of them might be helpful to refer to in setting up this game. Above all, remember that you are trying to create a game that helps participants understand a situation occurring in the real world. You are only simulating reality, making it simple so it can be better understood. You should keep in mind that the real situation is undoubtedly more complex and perhaps more difficult to understand.

Introduction

In this activity students form Constitutional Convention teams that cope creatively with serious issues that challenge countries thoughout the world. Each team will represent a different country for which it will write a constitution. The class then compares and contrasts the constitutions.

Objectives

Students will be able to:

- Understand why nations create constitutions To become aware of key global issues.
- Learn the difficulties involved in writing a constitution that fairly represents all of a nation's people.
- Compare and contrast various world constitutional models.

Grade Level

9-12

Time

One week

Materials

Copies of various countries' constitutions. Resource: Albert P. Blaustein and Gilbert H. Flanz, eds. <u>Constitutions of the Countries of the World.</u> Oceana Publications, Inc. Dobbs Ferry, NY.

Procedure

<u>Day 1</u>

1. Divide students into four teams, each one to write a constitution for a different country. Explain that each team must research the problems of the nation it represents before it can write that country's constitution. Suggest some typical worldwide problems (e.g., inflation, hunger, illiteracy, political instability) such nations may face.

2. Ask each group to list on paper as many problems as they can think of that have not yet been solved by the nation they represent. Allow students library research time before they begin their lists.

3. Post the lists on a bulletin board. Ask each group to explain its list to the class and to answer questions from other class members. Have other class members suggest additions to the lists.

4. Distribute constitutions copied from the Blaustein and Flanz book. Each team should only receive the constitution which concerns its nation.

5. Allow the teams class time in which to read the constitutions, or assign the reading as homework. After they have read the constitutions ask students if they have any questions concerning the documents, for example, about vocabulary.

<u>Day 2</u>

Have students rewrite their national constitutions to meet the problems of their societies as identified by their group lists.

<u>Day 3</u>

Allow time for student groups to complete the revision of their national constitutions.

<u>Day 4</u>

Have one person from each team read aloud the constitution for each nation. Other class members should ask questions and comment on whether each team sufficiently addressed the problems first identified as troubling the nation.

Debriefing

- Why are constitutions necessary? Why are laws and government necessary?

- What do the various constitutions which you revised say about the values of the people who wrote them?

- How were the constitutions similar in form? How did they differ?

- What specific issues did the constitutions cover? Which issues or problems should they address?

- How feasible would it be for various nations around the world to hold new Constitutional Conventions?

Follow-up

Distribute copies of your country's constitution. After the class has read it, ask how they would rewrite it to meet the needs of your society in the year 2010.

©CTIR
University of Denver

Introduction Students will become more aware of global interdependence and the complexities involved in resolving problems that affect more than one nation by participating in a simulated conference of the Organization of African Unity (OAU), an organization comprised of the continental African countries and islands surrounding Africa. Specific issues and problems are given for students to debate and resolve during the conference.

Objectives Students will be able to:

• Recognize the interdependence of the world's nations.
• Better understand the complexities and far-reaching effects of world problems.
• Become aware of international organizations, the way in which they function, and their effectiveness.
• Determine what factors result in power or a lack thereof.
• Identify global "actors," such as nations that may influence an issue or event.
• Learn how to promote one's viewpoint.
• Identify the positive and negative consequences of a decision.
• Generate realistic alternatives.
• Evaluate the quality and accuracy of information.

Grade Level 7-12

Time Three to eight class periods

Materials Handout #25, "Role Sheet"
Handout #26, "Assignment and Research Guide"
Handout #27, "Map of Africa"
Handout #28, "AIDS In Africa"
Handout #29, "Agenda"
Handout #30, "Text for Chairperson"
Handout #31, "Student Evaluation"
Typewriters (optional)
Name tags
Tape

Procedure 1. Explain to students they will split into pairs and each pair will be assigned an African country to research and represent as a member of the Organization of African Unity Council. Students should be told the conference's purpose is to solve crisis situations and decide major issues that affect African nations. Although working in pairs, students should understand they will be graded individually. You will also need to appoint students to the roles of chairperson, cochairperson, secretary, and newspaper reporters. You can base your choice of the African countries students will represent not only on

©CTIR
University of Denver

Handout #26, but on the current events and specific countries or issues your class has recently studied.

2. Distribute Handout #25. Write the names of the students who will represent specific nations beside the nation listed on the handout. In addition, list the names of students who will play chairperson, cochairperson, secretary, and reporters.

3. Distribute Handout #26 to each student. Discuss with the class what is expected of them and how they will be graded.

4. Distribute Handout #27.

5. Distribute Handout #28 showing the different countries of Africa and the incidence of AIDS.

6. Distribute Handout #29 so students can research and become familiar with issues to be discussed. (Issues may vary according to current events, topics studied in class, and your own preference. You may wish to make up some of the issues; they do not have to be actual problems that are happening in Africa today.) Allow students time to read the handout.

7. Give each reporter a name tag on which to write the name of the publication s/he represents. If possible, provide two or three typewriters on which the reporters can prepare stories, editorials, and newsbriefs.

8. Tell the student journalists they are to report on the events, issues, proposals, and decisions made during the conference. They may interview council members and report on caucus proceedings. The typewriters should be used right in the conference room and reports should be taped on the wall as soon as completed. Encourage all students participating in this activity to write editorials and give interviews. Remind students that because most countries are represented by two members, they should take advantage of this situation. While one member represents a nation at the conference table, the partner can give a statement or interview to the press. The partner could also write an editorial or negotiate with other representatives not at the conference table.

9. Instruct the secretary to take notes on the debate and vote on each agenda issue.

10. Have the chairperson call the conference to order and read aloud Handout #30. The chairperson will then follow the agenda, reading each issue or proposal aloud before opening it to debate. The chairperson and cochairperson must decide when a proposal should be voted on. They also must consider when and whether a caucus should be called to rewrite a proposal or to decide what the vote will be on the proposal. Caucuses can also be called for the purpose of writing a

proposal to resolve a problem brought out in an issue statement on the agenda. If a new proposal is written, it must be submitted to the chairperson. All proposals must be passed by a three-fourth's majority.

Debriefing

- How realistic was this simulation? In what ways was the conference realistic? Unrealistic?

- Discuss what made the conference unrealistic. Is there any way for the OAU to enforce decisions and policies it makes? Are these methods effective?

- How were decisions made?

- What kinds of negotiations and trades occurred beyond the conference table?

- Why did some nations have more power and influence than others?

- Did interdependence with other African nations affect decisions? How?

- Did you promote your own interests and conscience or those of the nation you represented?

- How feasible is it for a political representative to vote according to his/her conscience?

- Is it difficult to be the voice for a nation? How does it feel?

- Does a nation really speak as one voice?

- How does one promote and represent the interests of a nation?

- What local, national, and global actors (people, nations, and organizations) exert influence?

- Why do some actors have more impact on decisions than do others?

- What are the pressures a statesman would have to face when representing a nation in an international organization?

- As you played your roles, did you really feel some of those pressures?

- In what ways could a statesman be torn as to the course of action to follow?

- Discuss the power of nations as opposed to the power of international organizations such as the OAU and the United Nations (UN). (This may require some additional research.)

- Are international organizations like the UN and OAU basically nonpowerful? In what ways and why? What can they accomplish?

- If international organizations seem to be endowed with little power, then what is their purpose? Can they serve any worthwhile cause?

- Do they serve as a forum for debate and discussion? Is that useful?

- What would have to happen in order for the OAU or the UN to enforce policy?

- OPEC is an international organization. Is it more influential than an organization like the OAU or the UN? In what ways and why?

- In addition to international organizations such as the OAU and UN, identify other global actors that may influence world events.

- Discuss the influence and power multinational corporations exert on the global scene.

- How does trade affect national and global situations?

- How accurate is research?

- What affects the accuracy of information?

- Is there such a thing as objective news?

- Does the source and time from which information came have anything to do with the information's objectivity or accuracy?

- What were some of the frustrations you experienced in trying to obtain information?

Follow-up

After the conference and debriefing, ask students to turn in their research, news reports, and editorials. Distribute Handout #31 and have students complete the questionnaire.

Suggested Newsbriefs Related to Agenda Issues

Issue 1. While observing the students debate this issue, look for the student who argues most intensely for the sale of oil at reduced prices to underdeveloped African nations. Interrupt the debate so a reporter can announce that a large amount of oil has been discovered in that country. It is interesting to note if the student will reverse his/her argument.

A newsbrief could also announce the discovery of oil on the border of two countries. Somalia and Kenya are good examples because they have a traditional border dispute. It centers on the Shiftra Movement where northern Kenya is claimed by Somalians. Terrible atrocities are committed by both parties, and people and cattle are often shot on sight.

Issue 6. A reporter should announce that Rwandan rebels have attacked a UN refugee camp and have taken 150 hostages, most of them relief workers. A number of the hostages are workers from African nations.

NOTE: These issues and newsbriefs are only suggestions. They can be added to, rearranged, or deleted. They may be made more complicated or simplified according to the age group involved. Other issues could involve the following: pollution of Lake Victoria; aid to nations suffering drought; a trade embargo on South Africa; the harnessing of hydroelectric power; an oil spill, and so on.

Resource: It is suggested that the school library order "Background Notes" from the Department of State for each African nation. These may be obtained from: Department of State Publications 8032, Office of Media Services, Bureau of Public Affairs, Superintendent of Documents, U.S. Government Printing Office, Washington, DC 20402.

ROLE SHEET

Algeria	Mali
Angola	Mauritania
Benin	Mauritius
Botswana	Morocco
Burkina Faso	Mozambique
Burundi	Namibia
Cameroon	Niger
Cape Verde Islands	Nigeria
Central African Republic	Reunion
Chad	Rwanda
Comoros Islands	Sao Tome & Principe
Congo	Senegal
Cote d'Ivoire	Seychelles Islands
Djibouti	Sierra Leone
Egypt	Somalia
Equatorial Guinea	South Africa
Ethiopia	Sudan
Gabon	Swaziland
The Gambia	Tanzania
Ghana	Togo
Guinea	Tunisia
Guinea-Bissau	Uganda
Kenya	Western Sahara
Lesotho	Zaire
Liberia	Zambia
Libya	Zanzibar
Madagascar	Zimbabwe
Malawi	

ASSIGNMENT AND RESEARCH GUIDE

Write at least one page of information about the country you were assigned to represent. All students, including the chairperson, cochairperson, secretary, and reporters, should briefly research the issues listed on the conference agenda. Students who represent specific countries should compare their agenda research to the research reports concerning their individual nations. Become as familiar as possible with your country and the issues to be covered in the conference. You will be graded on individual research, participation, and overall behavior. At the end of the conference you will have the opportunity to evaluate yourself, other class members, and the worth of this activity.

Requirements:

Research should be at least one page in length, all items subtitled. Country must be researched as well as issues on agenda.

Make a bibliography using a variety of resources, i.e., encyclopedias, books, magazines, and clipped newspaper articles.

Draw free-hand a map of the country you are to represent.

Make a name tag for your country.

In studying individual countries, research the following information:

1. Historical background (enemies, friends)
2. Resources (Are they exported or used internally? How valuable?)
3. Major trading partners and products
4. Military status (size, nuclear power access)
5. Type of agricultural products
6. Population
7. Transportation system (rail, air, water, canal, river, port)
8. Major cities and locations
9. Political situation (revolutionaries)
10. Problems and weaknesses

Reporters, please turn in all news reports at the end of the conference. Be sure you place your name at the top right hand corner.

All editorials will also be turned in at the end of the conference

©CTIR
University of Denver

MAP OF AFRICA

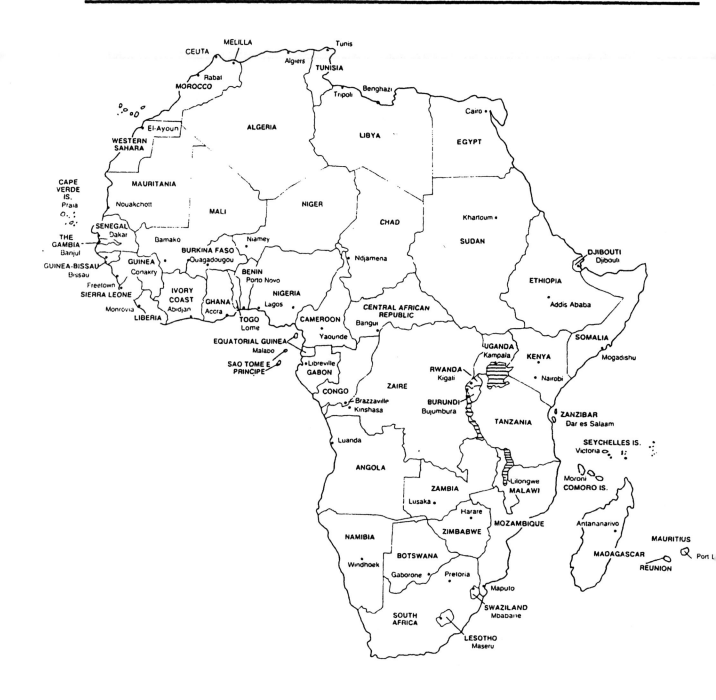

108

AIDS IN AFRICA

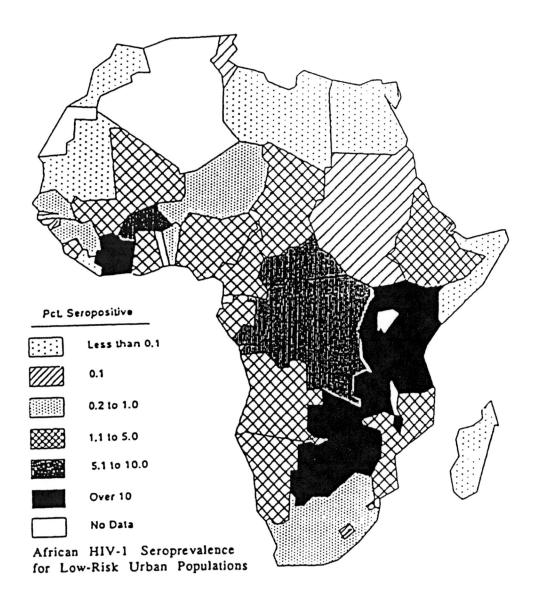

PcL Seropositive

Less than 0.1

0.1

0.2 to 1.0

1.1 to 5.0

5.1 to 10.0

Over 10

No Data

African HIV-1 Seroprevalence
for Low-Risk Urban Populations

Reprinted with permission. *World Eagle*, November, 1993. 1-800-854-8273.

AGENDA

Issue 1 - Proposal

It is proposed that African countries who have more oil than they can use will sell oil at lower prices (at least a 10 percent reduction) to underdeveloped African countries.

Issue 2 - Proposal

A task force appointed by the OAU will be set up for the primary purpose of controlling and eventually eliminating AIDS. Each member nation will be expected to donate one-half of 1 percent of their GNP for this program.

Issue 3

A European country has been granted permission by Zaire to build a military base in the Katanga region, located in southeast Zaire. The base will be equipped with a sophisticated weapons system and will also be the site for an experimental missile. Neighboring countries of Zaire, particularly Angola, Zambia, and Tanzania are angered and totally disapprove of this plan for a foreign military base. They want sanctions brought against Zaire.

Issue 4

OAU military will help to stabilize the situation in Liberia by working with the current government and the rebels to hold elections by January 1995. The elections will be supervised by the OAU or United Nations representatives.

Issue 5 - Proposal

Many member nations of the OAU have expressed that there is a great need to adopt one language to be learned and spoken by all people throughout Africa. Of all the languages spoken in Africa, five have been determined as the ones most common. Therefore, it is proposed that one of the five should be made the universal language of Africa. A vote will be made to adopt one of the following languages: Hausa, Swahili, French, English, or Arabic.

Issue 6

Rwandan refugees are fleeing across the border into Zaire and there is a need to take care of them. The United Nations will be stopping their food shipments shortly and the refugees need to be relocated from the camps to more permanent settlements. It is proposed that each of the African nations contribute toward the cost of resettlement.

Issue 7

Hundreds of people have been imprisoned, tortured and murdered under the politically repressive regime of Zaire's leader Mobutu Sese-Seku. As a result of the wide-spread reports of the massacre of protesting Lumbumbashi University students, it is proposed that the OAU recognize and condemn Mobutu for violating the human rights of Zairean citizens.

Issue 8

The African Commission on Human and Peoples' Rights should investigate the problem of expulsion of migratory laborers. Specifically, recently the Nigerian government has expelled hundreds of Ghanans from Nigeria because they felt that the Ghanans were employed in positions that should only be held by Nigerians.

Issue 9

The Mbuti Pygmy tribe living in the Ituri Forest in northeast Zaire, as well as other scattered Pygmy tribes throughout the rain forests of the Central African Republic and Cameroon, are threatened by extinction. It is estimated that Pygmies need two and one-half square miles per person for survival. Anthropologists believe that if nothing is done to provide for the survival of these people that by the year 2000 there will be no more left.

TEXT FOR CHAIRPERSON

TO BE READ BY THE CHAIRPERSON (the first day of conference only)

The conference of the Organization of African Unity will come to order (use gavel).

This conference is now in session. The secretary will call roll. Answer present when your country's name is called. (Secretary does this.)

I will remind council members of the rules governing this conference. No one will speak unless given permission by the chairperson. Two countries may debate at the table if given permission by the chairperson, however, the chairperson will break into the debate or end it if representatives cannot conduct themselves in a proper manner. Please raise your hand and speak only when acknowledged by the chairperson. State your business clearly and concisely and then sit down. Rudeness to the chairperson will not be tolerated. When the chairperson calls for order, it will be enforced immediately. If a member of this council should interrupt the order of this conference too often, he will forfeit his vote and he will be removed from the table until the next issues is brought forth. When the chairperson grants a caucus, no one has the floor, all members are free to discuss the issues among themselves. A caucus is usually called for the purpose of members deciding how they will vote on an issue or for members to discuss and present a proposal when the meeting is called to order.

The purpose of this conference is to find solutions to crisis situations and make decisions regarding major issues affecting African nations. The council is authorized to carry out proposals voted on and passed by a majority of council members. All is done in the interest of making a better Africa.

STUDENT EVALUATION

1. Was this activity worthwhile? Why or why not?

2. What did you learn?

3. What did you like best about this activity?

4. What did you like least about this activity?

5. Why did some nations have more power and influence than others?

6. Did interdependence with other African nations affect decisions? How?

7. Did students promote their own interests and conscience, or those of the nation they represented?

8. How feasible is it for a political representative to vote according to his/her conscience?

9. Is it difficult to be the voice for a nation? How does it feel?

10. Does a nation really speak as one voice?

11. How does one promote and represent the interests of a nation?

12. What local, national, and global actors (people, nations, and organizations) exert influence?

13. Why do some actors have more impact on decisions than others?

14. What are the pressures a statesman would have to face when representing a nation in an international organization?

15. As you played your roles, did you really feel some of those pressures?

16. In what ways could a statesman be torn as to the course of action to follow?

17. How accurate is research?

18. What affects the accuracy of information?

19. Is there such a thing as objective news?

20. Does the source and time from which information comes have anything to do with the information's objectivity or accuracy?

21. What were some of the frustrations you experienced in trying to obtain information?

22. Did you play your role well? Explain your answer.

23. Did you feel you excelled in any aspect of the activity? Explain.

24. Were you ever frustrated or uncertain about how to participate in the imaginary conference?

25. Was there any time when you were confused?

26. What suggestions can you give that would improve this activity?

27. Evaluate the person with whom you worked if you represented a country. Briefly describe their cooperation, participation, and overall contribution.

28. Evaluate the chairman and cochairman as to how well they participated and played their roles.

IV. HUMAN RIGHTS

Introduction

Maps can provide a variety of information in addition to physical contours, geographical relationships, and political boundaries. Sometimes visual illustrations of data are easier to understand and have more impact than lists of statistics.

In this activity students will create their own world maps based on data concerning military expenditures and socioeconomic indicators such as gross national product (GNP), population growth rate, and literacy rate. By deliberately distorting maps of various regions of the world to represent the data about those areas, students will develop a greater awareness of the disparities of resources, wealth, and power in the international system.

Traditionally we have accepted the GNP as the total amount of goods and services produced annually by a nation and the primary indicator of whether a nation's living standards are improving. Does the nation with the highest GNP or the highest per capita GNP (the amount of goods and services produced per person) necessarily have the highest quality of life? What other factors or conditions determine quality of life, and how do different regions of the world compare with regard to these indicators? Does a high rate of military spending improve a country's standard of living? Is social welfare often sacrificed for military strength?

Upon completing their maps, students will compare and contrast the quality of life around the world and will reach conclusions as to their definition of quality of life.

Objectives

Students will be able to:

• Analyze and use information from charts and graphs.
• Reproduce statistical information visually in the form of world and community maps.
• Consider different socioeconomic indicators that contribute to the quality of life and to formulate a definition of this concept.
• Develop a greater awareness of disparities of wealth, power, and quality of life around the world.

Grade Level 11-12

Time Two class periods

Materials
Handout #32, "World Map"
Handout #33, "Global Data Charts"
Handout #34, "Regional Groupings"
Handout #35, "Distorted World Maps"

Procedure 1. Distribute Handout #32.

2. Divide the class into groups and have each group choose a chart from Handout #33. Direct each group to draw a map of the world based only on the information provided in the charts. Tell them to distort the sizes of the landmasses to visually represent the data.

3. Discuss the concept of "scale" in map making. How can students visually depict the information on the charts? How can they show the relative differences between countries? Students need not be overly concerned with outlining the political boundaries between nation-states. The names of the countries included in each regional grouping appear on Handout #34. Ask students whether, in regard to specific indicators (e.g., GNP or literacy rate), they think there can be a great disparity between different countries in the same regional group.

4. Distribute Handout #35. It is a good example of map distortion that illustrates world supply and demand. Tell students to keep this example in mind, but also urge them to be creative. This part of the activity may be started during one class period and continued as a homework assignment.

5. In class, prominently display the completed maps, but cover the maps' titles so they cannot be seen. Have students guess what information they think each map visually represents.

6. Uncover the titles of the maps and discuss:

• What are the similarities and differences of the maps?

• Which regions of the world are distorted to sizes larger than their actual physical boundaries? To sizes smaller?

• Is there continuity in the distortions? Are the maps correctly drawn to scale?

• What do the maps suggest about the quality of life in different areas of the world? Does there appear to be a relationship between GNP and other quality of life indicators, such as life expectancy and literacy rate?

• What sort of relationship might exist between a high level of military spending and the quality of life?

• How would population pressures affect economic well-being and the quality of life?

• Are there other indicators of quality of life which are not depicted by these maps? What other indicators do you think should be included?

- If you lived in Latin America, what quality of life problem would you be most anxious to change? Explain. What would you change if you lived in North America? In Russia?

Debriefing

- How would you define the phrase "quality of life?"

- How would you compare the quality of life in your country to other countries?

- How many statements can you make in comparing the various data presented (e.g., do infant mortality and literacy rates correlate to the GNP or are the most populated countries also the most powerful ones)? List these statements on the chalkboard.

Follow-up

1. Write a 250 word essay defining quality of life.

2. In groups of five, write a group paper on "The Quality of Life: United States vs. Other Countries."

Additional Activities

The following exercise is adapted from an activity entitled "Measuring the Quality of Life" that appeared in Intercom 82: Environmental Issues and the Quality of Life. Global Perspectives in Education, 1976, p. 15.

1. Ask students how they would measure the quality of life in their community and represent it on a map. Encourage them to research information about what contributes to and what detracts from quality of life in their community. Ask students what indicators they think are important to observe.

2. Have students decide what indicators they want to research. Encourage them to be specific, accurate, and methodical. They should seek statistics that can be illustrated visually.

For example, to investigate social quality of life the following information could be obtained: percent of households with telephones; percent of workers using public transportation; cost of living index; number of swimming pools per 100,000 people; sports events in local area; percent of unemployed; percent of blacks unemployed; percent of women unemployed.

Information can be obtained by calling or writing local community government offices, libraries, and agencies such as the Chamber of Commerce. Other helpful sources are newspaper files, The Statistical Abstract of the U.S. (published annually), and the County and City Guidebook (U.S. Government publications).

3.When students have compiled their information, instruct them to present it in the form of a map. Display and evaluate the maps.

Debriefing

- What are the strengths and weaknesses of this community mapping survey?

- What do the maps tell you about your community? What information was omitted?

- How do you evaluate the quality of life in your community? (Rate it on a scale of 1-10.)

- How does it compare to the quality of life in different regions of the world? In Latin America? In Russia?

- If people in our country did more to help others, how would this affect the quality of your life?

- What could we do to help others living in less fortunate communities? Is it our responsibility to do this?

Follow-up

Ask students how they think their community's quality of life will change in the next twenty years. How will the global quality of life be altered? Have them write short papers on what indicators they perceive will be the most important in determining the quality of life in the year 2000.

©CTIR
University of Denver

WORLD MAP

GLOBAL DATA CHARTS

POPULATION ESTIMATE, MID-1994
(Millions)

South Asia	1,812
East Asia	1,414
Africa	700
Europe	728
Latin America	470
United States	261
Western Asia	165
Canada	29
Australia	18

INFANT MORTALITY RATE*

Africa	92
South Asia	72
Western Asia	56
Latin	49
Asia	29
Europe	11
United States	8.3
Canada	6.8
Australia	6.6

*Infant death per 1,000 live births

MILITARY EXPENDITURES PER CAPITA 1990
(Millions of U.S. dollars)

United States	1,097
Western Asia	560
Canada	339
Australia	271
Europe	264
East Asia	167
Latin America	31
Africa	29
South Asia	20

1994 World Population Data Sheet, Population Reference Bureau, Inc., and World Military and Social Expenditures 1993, Ruth E. Sivard, World Priorities Inc, Washington, D.C.

©CTIR
University of Denver

GNP PER CAPITA 1992
(US dollars)

United States	23,120
Canada	20,320
Australia	17,070
Europe	11,990
East Asia	3,200
Latin America	2,710
Western Asia	2,680
South Asia	1,090
Africa	650

PRIMARY SCHOOL AGE POPULATION IN SCHOOL
(Percentage ages 5-11)

United States	99
Australia	98
Canada	97
Europe	93
East Asia	93
Western Asia	89
Latin America	86
South Asia	71
Africa	57

LITERACY RATE*
(F/M)

United States	99/99
Australia	98/98
Canada	97/97
Europe	96/98
Latin America	83/87
East Asia	70/87
Western Asia	45/69
Africa	42/61
South Asia	32/59

*Percentage of adult population over 15 years able to read and write

LIFE EXPECTANCY AT BIRTH (Years)

Canada	77
Australia	77
United States	76
Europe	73
Latin America	68
East Asia	67
Western Asia	61
South Asia	58
Africa	55

PUBLIC HEALTH EXPENDITURES PER CAPITA
(in millions of U.S. Dollars)

Canada	1,123
United States	1,012
Europe	915
Australia	563
East Asia	86
Western Asia	50
Latin America	28
Africa	10
South Asia	3

PERCENTAGE OF POPULATION WITH SAFE DRINKING WATER SUPPLY

United States	100
Australia	99
Europe	98
Canada	97
Western Asia	81
South Asia	80
Latin America	77
East Asia	73
Africa	47

NUMBER OF YEARS TO DOUBLE POPULATION
(at Current Rate)

Europe	1,025
United States	98
Canada	98
Australia	85
East Asia	51
Latin America	35
South Asia	33
Western Asia	26
Africa	24

REGIONAL GROUPINGS

Latin America	Europe
Antigua & Barbuda	Albania
Argentina	Austria
Bahamas	Belarus
Barbados	Belgium
Belize	Bosnia-Herzegovina
Bolivia	Bulgaria
Brazil	Croatia
Colombia	Czech Republic
Costa Rica	Denmark
Cuba	Estonia
Dominica	Finland
Dominican Republic	France
Ecuador	Germany
El Salvador	Greece
Grenada	Hungary
Guadeloupe	Iceland
Guatemala	Ireland
Guyana	Italy
Haiti	Latvia
Honduras	Liechtenstein
Jamaica	Lithuania
Martinique	Luxembourg
Mexico	Macedonia
Netherlands Antilles	Malta
Nicaragua	Moldova
Panama	Netherlands
Paraguay	Norway
Peru	Poland
Puerto Rico	Portugal
St. Kitts-Nevis	Romania
Saint Lucia	Russia
St. Vincent & the Grenadines	San Marino
Suriname	Slovakia
Trinidad & Tobago	Slovenia
Uruguay	Spain
Venezuela	Sweden
	Switzerland
	Ukraine
	United Kingdom
	Yugoslavia

Groupings according to 1994 World Population Data Sheet, Population Reference Bureau.

124

South Asia

Afghanistan
Bangladesh
Bhutan
Brunei
Cambodia
India
Indonesia
Iran
Kazahkhstan
Kyrgyzstan
Laos
Malaysia
Maldives
Myanmar
Nepal
Pakistan
Philippines
Singapore
Sri Lanka
Tajikistan
Thailand
Turkmenistan
Uzbekistan
Viet Nam

United States

Canada

East Asia

China
Hong Kong
Japan
Korea, North
Korea, South
Macao
Mongolia
Taiwan

Australia

Western Asia

Armenia
Azerbijan
Bahrain

Western Asia (cont)

Cyprus
Gaza
Georgia
Iraq
Israel
Jordan
Kuwait
Lebanon
Oman
Qatar
Saudi Arabia
Syria
Turkey
United Arab Emirates
West Bank
Yemen

Africa

Algeria
Angola
Benin
Botswana
Burkina Faso
Burundi
Cameroon
Cape Verde
Central African Republic
Chad
Comoros
Congo
Cote d'Ivoire
Djibouti
Equatorial Guinea
Ethiopia
Gabon
Gambia
Ghana
Guinea
Guinea-Bissau
Kenya
Lesotho
Liberia
Libya
Madagascar
Malawi
Mali

Africa (cont)

Mauritania
Mauritius
Morocco
Mozambique
Namibia
Niger
Nigeria
Reunion
Rwanda
Sao Tome & Principe
Senegal
Seychelles
Sierra Leone
Somalia
South Africa
Sudan
Swaziland
Tanzania
Togo
Tunisia
Uganda
Western Sahara
Zaire
Zambia
Zimbabwe

DISTORTED WORLD MAP

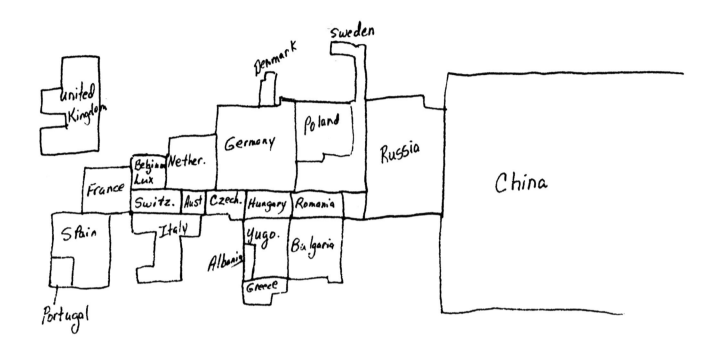

Smoking

Introduction	Many students have no conception of political repression. They do not understand the fear or inactivity of those whose rights have been suppressed. This "why don't they _do_ something" attitude needs to be tempered with an understanding of just what goes on in these peoples' lives. This human rights simulation will help students feel the fear and indecision facing people who live in politically repressive states. Hopefully, it will also give them an appreciation of the freedoms in their own country. (_Hope_: this simulation has a definite Latin American tint to it, but this does not mean that Latin America has a monopoly on human rights violations, nor that all Latin American governments are repressive.)
Objective	Students will be able to:

* Define the concept of "political rights."
* Simulate the psychological and physical pressure of political repression.
* Draw conclusions about the impact of domestic and global counter pressure on a repressive government.

Grade Level	7-12
Time	One class period
Materials	Handout #36, "Juan Verdad: Editor" Handout #37, "Roles" Handout #39, "Missing Narrative" Handout #40, "Supremia Herald"
Procedure	1. Discuss the meaning of the word "rights." What is a right? Who has rights? What are human rights? On the chalkboard write: Political, Economic, and Social. What are the rights that fit into these three categories? Do African countries place more importance on economic rights than political rights? Why? Which rights are most important for Central and South America? Why? Look at the list of political rights. Ask: Do all countries have political rights? Which countries do? Do not? 2. Explain to student that they are going to take part in a simulation about political rights. Distribute Handout #36 and read it out loud. Then distribute Handout #37 and read it aloud. Make sure that students understand what is expected of them.

Originally in Teaching About World Cultures, CTIR, University of Denver.

128

3. Assign roles to each student, Handout #38. Double up on some roles if necessary, e.g., social workers, nuns, priests, sons, daughters. Name tags might help students to keep track of everyone. Give students time to study their roles.

4. Read the narrative of Handout #39 out loud to students. Whenever it reaches "What should you do next?," carefully review the options available to the students, but do not tell them the consequences until after they have decided. Remind students to stay in their "roles" when making their decisions. Some students may prefer to think up their own options. In that case, the teacher will have to decide what the consequences should be.

During the second set of options, some students might choose Option A and will end up missing. Tell them to stand in a separate part of the classroom until they return to the game later in the narrative. During the very last set of options, many of the students will end up in jail. Keep those in jail separate from those who are missing, and also separate them from those who are still free.

5. When the narrative calls for it, distribute Handout #40 to everyone, regardless of their status. It contains information that will be useful to students in the discussion following the end of the game.

6. At the end of the simulation, arbitrarily release one-half of the jailed participants. During the evaluation questions, leave the jailed searchers separate from the freed searchers so that the students can visualize the simulation's ending.

Debriefing

- Why do you suppose the simulation ends here? Who is still in jail? What has changed since the simulation began? Does the ending make any sense?

- What has happened to the Indigis (the ones whose rights were originally suppressed)? Are they any better off? Will they ever be any better off? In the simulation, which story did the media cover, Verdad's disappearance or the Indigi massacres? Why? Can you think of any real life cases in which native people are suppressed (e.g., U.S., Australia, Brazil, South Africa, Romania)?

- List the rights which were denied in the simulation. What type of rights are they? Why do you think the authorities had to take the action they did? Are governments ever justified in denying political rights? In which cases? Would people with money have any of their rights denied? If they were put in jail would they have a greater chance of getting out because of money and/or influence?

- Were there any risks which had "good" consequences? (You may have to examine both the option-consequences sections, as well as the narrative itself.) Which risks had consequences that were "okay"? Which did not?

- Was it hard to figure out which options to choose? Did the decisions become easier to make once you had figured out what the government response would be? If you had lived in such a country all your life, how would this affect your political life? Would you <u>ever</u> take risks?

- Which factors were the most important leading to Verdad's eventual release? Least important? Was Supremian pressure more important than domestic pressure? What does this say about the foreign policy of powerful countries? Do individuals in powerful countries have a responsibility to individuals in smaller, repressive countries? Why or why not?

- Was this simulation realistic? How might money have an effect on the outcome? Does this simulation remind you of any real life situations? Would you like to live in Barbarica? Why or why not? Have your feelings about life in your own country changed? How?

Follow-up

1. Have students read books about human rights violations (check the bibliography for some references). Have a class discussion about the books, or have students write a report analyzing which rights were denied, what actions were taken, and who was or should have been responsible for alleviating the problems.

2. Have students collect news articles about human rights violations and their country's response to them. What factors prevent the country from acting?

JUAN VERDAD: EDITOR

Juan Verdad is the editor of Barbarica's largest news magazine, <u>Important Times</u>. He is very concerned about the impact of domestic and foreign investment on the well-being of Barbarica's people. Wealthy foreign and Barbarican investors want to develop the mineral-rich land in the unexplored interior of the country. Juan discovered that members of the Indigi tribe, who live on the land, are being threatened to get off the land, and in some cases, tortured or murdered.

Juan published this story in his magazine revealing the atrocities. He hinted strongly that foreign and domestic investors, along with the national government, might be responsible.

The day after the story was published, Juan Verdad and two assistant editors from <u>Important Times</u> disappeared. The government denied knowledge of their whereabouts. Verdad's family and friends decide to look for him.

RULES & GUIDELINES

1. <u>Your objective is to find Juan Verdad</u>. Remember: at times you must take chances in order to get information or to pressure the authorities. On the other hand, if you're in jail, you can't help to find Juan.

2. When the narrator reads the consequence of your choice, <u>react to the consequence</u> when the next set of options is read.

3. <u>Listen carefully to the story</u>. A case such as this is very complex; there are many actors and forces at work. Try to analyze people's actions as the story unfolds.

IMPORTANT ACTORS IN THE STORY

Juan Verdad, editor of <u>Important Times</u>

Jose Bolochet, President of Barbarica

Gerald Lewis, President of Supremia

James McPatrick, Supremian Ambassador to Barbarica

<u>Newtime</u>-a relatively conservative Supremian newsmagazine

<u>Supremia Herald</u>-a relatively liberal newspaper

Humongous International (HI), a Supremia-based multinational corporation with worldwide mining interests

Barbarican Council for Peace and Justice (BCPJ), an underground resistance movement

Indigi Tribe, poor native Barbaricans who live in the interior of the country

Amnesty International, an international organization devoted to curbing human rights abuses

©CTIR
University of Denver

ROLES

Juan's Mother: Your son has always been "into causes." You have spent most of your life worried for your son. Now, your worst fears have come true. You son is gone and his disappearance has put your whole family in jeopardy. You ask yourself at every decision: "Should I risk my family to find Juan?"	**Juan's Wife**: You and Juan discussed the possibility of him being kidnapped or killed and the two of you decided that the rest of the family should not be sacrificed for him. You love him, you miss him, but you keep your conversation in mind with every decision you are asked to make.
Juan's Son(s): All your life you have wanted to be like your father. You have championed every cause your father has taken up, often in a more vocal and spirited manner. Now your father is gone, and you vow to find him at all costs.	**Juan's Daughter(s)**: Your father is a very important person in your life, but your fiancé is an important government official. Your wedding is next month, and you don't want it jeopardized. You want to find your father, of course, but you take no risks that would publicize the disappearance too much.
Juan's Sister: Your brother has always been involved in causes, and he has always brought hardship and fear to the family. You knew this was coming, and you can't understand why he would continue to risk the family for causes that will not benefit the family at all.	**Juan's Brother(s)**: You want to find Juan, because he has always been a good brother and has always helped you out when you needed him. However, you have four children and a good job, so you consider these factors when you take any risk.
Indigi Social Worker(s): Juan has been a important ally in the fight for the Indigi cause against exploitation. You know that his disappearance is only the start of more suppression and hardship for the Indigis. You will use all your resources and take all risks to find Juan.	**Priest(s) and Nun(s)**:You have watched Juan champion many causes for all the impoverished people of Barbarica. His disappearance is a violation of freedom of speech, a basic human right, in your opinion. Therefore, you feel this should become an international incident, a calling card to all nations to fight political repression. You will take as many risks needed to make this incident internationally known.

133

International Journalist: Juan Verdad's disappearance is a deathblow to your profession and all that newspapers stand for--the dissemination of objective information, the guarding of people's rights against the government, the right to have opinions. You will take as many risks as necessary to keep freedom of the press alive.	**Domestic Journalist:** Juan has been your editor, so his disappearance complicates your life enormously, for you are now the one to make decisions about Important Times: what stories to cover, what to run in the paper, and how to report on Juan's disappearance. You realize that one wrong move may cause your own disappearance.
Local Mayor: Juan's family and magazine have helped you maintain your political office throughout the years. On the day Mrs. Verdad came to ask for help, you were also visited by a government official who asked you to work with the authorities. He offered you an appointment in the federal government, so every decision you make must take into account your alliance with the Verdad's as well as the benefits to your political career.	**Underground Activist(s):** Although never actually meeting Juan Verdad, he has been a champion of all your causes, so you will take as many covert risks as possible to aid Juan, both in jail and when he gets out.

TEACHER'S "MISSING" NARRATIVE

Verdad's family and friends decide to look for him. First they go to his office at Important Times. There they learn from Verdad's coworkers that he kept a special file containing revealing documents about the Indigi massacres. Upon opening the file, they find that the papers are gone.

WHAT SHOULD YOU DO NEXT?

A. Write a letter to the Barbarican government pleading for information about Verdad.

B. Write a news story/letter to the editor or give an interview to a news agency accusing the government of causing the disappearance of Verdad and the other two men.

C. Do nothing and keep quiet.

D. Own choice.

1 | For those choosing B: You are taken in by the police and interrogated. You are given a stern warning to avoid public action in. these matters. International Journalist never goes to jail in any consequence.

One Underground Activist is placed in jail and never let out, is not able to communicate with anyone, and no information is available to anyone.

Verdad's friends and family decide to visit the Director of Public Information. They ask him if he knows anything about Verdad, but he only repeats the government's position--that the national government has no knowledge of the disappearances.

WHAT SHOULD YOU DO NEXT?

A. Lead a demonstration in front of the Director of Public Information's Office.

B. Ask the Supremia Ambassador for help.

C. Go home and do nothing.

D. Own choice.

2 | For those choosing A: People involved in the demonstration are now missing. You are no longer part of the Verdad search.

For those choosing B: You are picked up by the police, beaten, interrogated, and released. They warn you not to get involved.

135

The Domestic Journalist, Indigi Social Worker, and any underground activists are sent to jail.

The two assistant editors are released from the city prison. They tell Verdad's family and friends that the last time they saw Verdad, he was being taken to another jail, but that he was indeed alive. However, he needed help from the guards to walk. The assistant editors assume that Verdad has been tortured. They warn everybody that the government will not tolerate efforts to direct public attention to the Verdad disappearance. In addition, the Supremia Ambassador to Barbarica grants an interview to a reporter which is printed in Newstime, a Supremia magazine. Here is an excerpt from the article:

> James McPatrick, Supremia's Ambassador in Barbarica, expressed today in a phone interview that the Supremia government has "full and unabashed confidence in the integrity of Humongous International and the Barbarican government." He did not mention the mysterious disappearance of Juan Verdad, editor of Important Times, nor did he comment on accusations that Verdad is being tortured by the government.

WHAT SHOULD YOU DO NEXT?

A. Contact the Barbarican Council for Peace and Justice.

B. Go to the jail and demand to see Verdad.

C. Go home and lock the door (i.e., "do nothing").

D. Own choice.   3

> If you choose A and are Priests or Nuns, you go to jail. For those Choosing B: You are locked up for 24 hours and beaten. You receive no food. The authorities do not charge you with anything, but warn you not to make any trouble. You are released and join Verdad's other friends who are contacting the BCPJ.

The leaders of the demonstration against the government are released and join Verdad's family and friends at an underground meeting. At the meeting, the people voice their fears about Verdad's well-being. They resolve to find him. Through a contact in the government, the Council members tell them that the government's policy against the Indigi people has been stepped up. They decide to start a worldwide campaign to put pressure on the Barbarican government, so they contact Amnesty International. They hope that the pressure will force the government to release Verdad and to stop the Indigi slaughter.

WHAT SHOULD YOU DO NEXT?

A. write a story/letter to the editor/provide information to a news agency/denouncing the Supremia government for doing nothing about the human rights violations in Barbarica.

B. Organize a boycott of Humongous International products sold in Barbarica.

C. Wait for governmental response to Amnesty International pressure (i.e., "do nothing").

D. Own choice

> 4 For those choosing A; You find your dog dead in the bushes near your home. A note is attached which says: "You're next." For those choosing B: You are picked up by the police and detained for 24 hours.

An important newspaper in Supremia, the Supremia Herald, prints Verdad's original story as well as an editorial accusing the Barbarican government of denying human rights, suggesting that Verdad's case may only be the tip of iceberg. This causes a great sensation in Supremia, and the citizens there pressure their politicians to do something. The Supremia Ambassador responds to this pressure with the following news release:

> Embassy Press------(Dateline) BARBARICA
> The nations of Supremia and Barbarica have a long history of solid relations. It is unfortunate that certain elements in Supremia choose to undermine that relationship with unfounded accusations. I have the utmost confidence that if there has been any wrongdoing, of which at this date there is no evidence, it will be investigated thoroughly.

Meanwhile Amnesty International letters pour into the Barbarican President's office. Although Verdad's friends and family are encouraged by the international pressure, the government continues to deny knowledge or responsibility of his absence. The government claims to have questioned some low-ranking officials, but Verdad's friends consider this as tokenism.

WHAT SHOULD YOU DO NEXT?

A. Organize a public demonstration in Barbarica's National Plaza.

B. Go visit the Director of Public Information again.

C. Do nothing. (Remind students they cannot "do nothing" twice in a row.)

D. Own Choice

> 5 For those choosing A or B: You are arrested and thrown in jail.

The Barbarican mass arrests cause an uproar in the Supremian media. Ambassador McPatrick requests a private meeting with the Barbarican President, Jose Bolochet. The Supremia Herald prints an editorial speculating about the content of the meeting. (Pass out Handout #53 and read it outloud.)

The next day Verdad is pushed out of a speeding car, weary, but alive. He is stripped of his post as editor of Important Times, and the government takes over the magazine. (Let one-half of the jailed participants out of prison.)

©CTIR
University of Denver

-SUPREMIA HERALD-

Editorial: By the Foreign Journalist

President Bolochet must feel like a chastised little boy as he returns to the presidential mansion after his meeting with Ambassador McPatrick. Becuase Supremia pays for three-quarters of Barbarica's total foreign aid package, the threat of aid suspension was probably dangled in front of Bolochet as a very real and effective means of altering Barbarican policy.

Until now, Supremia has been content to let the Barbaricans solve their own problems. Why should President Gerald Lewis' Administration suddenly car about a popular disturbance in a small country? In the first place, yesterday's mass arrests were no small "popular disturbance," but a clear violation of political rights. Further, President Lewis cares because the Supremian citizens care. The upcoming election, no doubt, has something to do with his increased responsiveness.

Bolochet has other powers to answer to than the Supremian Administration. Humongous International, a Supremia-based multinational corporation, is not known for investing in unstable countries. The recent disturbances in Barbarica make the corporate board very nervous. Bolochet need only recall IH's pullout from San Ruffia last year when labor riots in that nation destroyed many newly-dug mine shafts.

Amidst all the power politics, though, we only hope that the pressure on the Barbarican government does some good and that Juan Verdad is found alive.

HOW ARE YOU GOING TO KEEP THEM DOWN ON THE FARM?

Introduction   A typical phenomenon in a developing country is massive rural-urban migration, caused in part by economic disparities and urban cultural advantages. Some cities, such as Cairo, Egypt, Lagos, Nigeria, and Mexico City, Mexico, have experienced unusually rapid urban growth, causing problems with housing, sanitation, transportation, and social disintegration. China's government has recognized the serious consequences of a large influx of population into its cities and has tried a number of solutions in the past thirty years. In this activity, students use a case study and statistical data to make conclusions about the push-pull factors for the migration of Chinese peasants to the cities. Several alternative programs are presented for discouraging migration, and students are asked to choose one program and defend it. Class discussion then focuses on how these programs might be applied in other developing countries.

Objectives   Students will be able to:

- Analyze Chinese statistical and case study data for push-pull factors in rural-urban migration.
- Evaluate alternative Chinese programs to discourage migration.
- Apply these programs in the context of other developing countries.

Grade Level   9-12

Time   Two class periods

Materials   Handout #41, "Chinese Statistics"
Handout #42, "Case Study"
Handout #43, "Alternative Programs"

Procedure   1. Distribute Handout #41. Based on the statistics, ask students to compile a list of reasons why a Chinese peasant would want to move to a city. What factors would discourage him/her from wanting to move? Discuss their answers and explain that the statistics tell only part of the story. They will now read a case study to see how these figures translate into people's daily lives.

2. Distribute Handout #42 and have students read the case study. Ask students to add additional factors to each of their lists. Discuss and then ask for a vote on whether or not they would actually try to migrate to the city if they were Mei Xiao-lan. (The class will probably vote "yes," which gives the teacher an opportunity to make the transition to the next part of the activity.)

Adapted from Teaching About World Cultures: Focus on Developing Regions. CTIR. 1984.

3. Discuss possible problems that might result from massive rural-urban migration (unemployment, housing shortage, poor sanitation, inadequate transportation, rise in crime). Again refer students to Handout #41 to check the unemployment rate in China. Housing is extremely limited in Chinese cities, with an average of 3.6 sq. meters per person. Pollution, traffic jams, and crime have also been on the increase. If the class has studied other cities such as Mexico City, Mexico, Calcutta, India, Cairo, Egypt, Rio de Janiero, Brazil, Lagos, Nigeria, and Tokyo, Japan, refer to them as examples of potential problems if rural-urban migration in a developing country is unchecked.

4. The Chinese government has attempted a number of solutions to the migration problem during the past thirty years. Distribute Handout #43 which describes programs the government tried at various times. Ask the students to evaluate the programs based on their own criteria and to decide which they would recommend. This may be done by individuals or in small groups. Criteria may include any or all of the following: economic development of the country, social control, individual motivation, human rights, profit, and pragmatism.

Debriefing

- How can you justify your choice of programs based on the criteria you feel is most important?

- Are these criteria consistent with Chinese values today?

- Are the programs workable?

- What indications of success are there for any of the programs?

- Will the success be maintained over a longer period of time?

- How will China "keep them down on the farm?" Should they?

- Does a government have the right to make such decisions based on the argument that they are avoiding the problems of a Calcutta or a Mexico City?

Follow-up

Apply the concepts in the Chinese programs to other developing countries the class has studied. Which would probably work? Which could only work in China? What recommendations would the class make to other developing countries based on the Chinese experience?

CHINESE STATISTICS

COMPOSITION OF POPULATION

	1950	1978	1987
Total		962.6	1,080.7
Urban	6,096.4	172.5	503.6
Rural	49,379.1	790.1	577.1

COMPOSITION OF LABOR FORCE

	1957	1975	1987
	% of Total	% of Total	% of Total
Agriculture	84.5	76.7	30.1
Industry	15.5	23.3	19.9

PER CAPITA INCOME (in Yuan*)

	1977	1980	1987
Rural	65.40	118.50	462.60
Urban	411.50	569.90	1,012.20

URBAN UNEMPLOYMENT

1978	1987
5.30%	2.00%

TOTAL VALUE OF AGRICULTURAL OUTPUT

1977-81	18%
1981-87	47%
1988-91	8%

*On 1990 a Yuan was worth approximately $5.222 U.S.

Sources: China Statistical Abstract 1988 and China Facts and Figures Annual.

©CTIR
University of Denver

CASE STUDY

Mei Xiao-lan is a twenty-year-old member of a rural commune in South China, about thirty miles from the large city of Guangzhou.* She and her brother and sister spend much of their time working in the fields, tending their family's private plot, and taking care of the pigs and ducks that the family sells in the free market. Because there are five members of the family who are working, the Mei family is considered more prosperous than some of their neighbors, with a yearly income 800 Yuan (approximately $4,180 U.S.).

Xiao-lan has completed junior middle school (equivalent to a United States junior high school), which is as far as most rural students go. Her parents wanted her to go to work so that the family income would increase. Sometimes she envies her cousin in the city who is studying science in senior middle school, although she knows that her cousin may have to wait one or two years for a job after she graduates.

The Mei family is proud of their achievements in the past few years. Because they are close to the city, they can sell some of the vegetables, pigs, and ducks they raise there. This gives them a higher income than peasants in more remote areas. The family income has doubled in the past five yeas. Much of what they made has been invested in more animals, which in turn led to greater profits. Since the end of the Cultural Revolution in China, such "capitalism" by individual peasants is no longer frowned upon by the government, and they have been encouraged to expand their sideline activities.

This has not been without cost, however. More work means longer hours, sometimes up to ten to twelve hours per day, seven days a week during the busy season. In hot, humid South China, tasks such as planting rice seedlings in the flooded paddies can mean backbreaking work. Xiao-lan often thinks how much nicer it would be to have a factory job in the city with regular hours.

The family eats well, probably better than their city cousins who often cannot get as much of a variety of fresh vegetables. Xiao-lan remembers the leaner years, when the family only had meat on special occasions and the grain allocations were lower per family. Now, because they are raising their own animals, the family eats meat or poultry several times per week.

Xiao-lan's sister, who is eighteen, suffers from diabetes. She has difficulty getting medicine and must make the trip to the city several times a year to see a specialist, since none of the health workers in the commune are trained in this speciality.

In the evenings, Xiao-lan and her friends like to watch the family's TV, which they bought last year with some of their savings. It makes them feel closer to the life in cities such as

---

*   Guangzhou - Canton

Beijing, Shanghai, and Guangzhou, although it also reminds them how much fun it would be to be able to go to the movies or the theater in the city.

Next month Xiao-lan's cousin will come for a visit. It is the busy season on the commune, and the family will welcome an extra hand to work in the fields. Her cousin enjoys getting away from the heat and pollution of Guangzhou. She especially enjoys the Mei family's spacious home, which she says is much better than her family's cramped two-room apartment. Her parents cannot join her because as factory workers they do not get vacations except for a few national holidays.

Mei Xiao-lan thinks of her life on the farm as unglamorous, although she has a certain amount of economic security. She worries what will happen if next year the weather is bad or the government changes its policies. Will she marry a peasant and spend the rest of her life on the commune? Sometimes she wonders what her life would be like if she could trade places with her city cousin.

ALTERNATIVE PROGRAMS

Youth to the Countryside

In this program, millions of middle school (high school) graduates were sent to rural areas to help to counterbalance the increase in urban population. Many of them were sent to frontier provinces, where they helped in education and health programs as well as working in the fields. Because the growing number of middle school graduates had been a major cause of unemployment in the cities, this program helped to reduce the unemployment rate. The students had valuable skills to offer the peasants, who in turn taught them a very different style of life from that of the cities. Students gained greater respect for the peasants by actually taking part in farm labor and talking with them about the hardships of their life. Some students said that the experience gave them a greater appreciation for the many different ethnic and social groups that make up their country. They had a feeling of being an important part of "building socialism" in China, of helping the nation to develop. (U.S. students might compare some of the positive aspects of this program to the Peace Corps or similar domestic volunteer programs, although the Chinese students were by no means volunteers.) When the program was at its height, over two million urban youth were sent to the countryside each year. Many were unsure when, or if, they would be allowed to return to the city.

Commune Workshops

The basic idea of this program was to introduce industry into the rural areas; to give the peasants an understanding of what was involved in the manufacturing process and involve them in the national development effort. It was also thought that the program would make use of extra workers in the rural areas, increase peasant income, and prevent further migration to urban areas. Some of the original projects were quite ambitious. The most famous were the "backyard steel furnaces," primitive attempts to have peasants produce small quantities of steel. Most of these were abandoned within a few years. However, a number of other kings of workshops were introduced that did succeed in adding to commune income and providing needed products. For example, one commune had a peanut oil factory, brick kiln, furniture shop, and herbal medicine workshop. Peasants were trained to repair farm machinery and bicycles. Although the number of workers involved was a small percentage of the commune's population, this program was thought to give peasants a more active role in national development and to make them more self-reliant.

Responsibility System (Ziren zhi)

The basic idea of the Responsibility System is that peasant earnings are directly linked to output. Each family signs a contract to deliver part of what they produce to the state. They may keep whatever they produce above this quota or sell it at higher prices to the state. Under this system, collective labor as it was known before does not really exist. A family that works harder and produces more, even though they do it on government-owned land, receives a higher income. Some families have begun to specialize in certain crops,

144

especially those near urban areas who can get high prices for poultry, tobacco, and other products. With their new profits, peasants are buying consumer products such as bicycles, tape recorders and television sets. Some are building new homes. The agricultural output nationwide exhibited a marked increase in the first three years of the program, but there was concern that inequities, both within communes and among regions, would widen. Critics asked what had become of the old socialist maxim, "From each according to his ability. To each according to his need." Wealthy regions and families with many active workers would prosper, while more remote and infertile regions, and families with fewer resources would find their position deteriorating.

Urban Identification Booklet (Hukou System)

A _hukou_ is a small paper booklet in which members of each urban household are registered. Without a hukou, one cannot receive food rations, a job, or housing. Before a peasant can move to the city (or a youth sent to the countryside can return to the city), he or she must first receive a hukou from the government. During the 1970s this was very difficult to accomplish. Periodic checks of urban neighborhoods by neighborhood committee officials or police still locate peasants without hukou who are subsequently ordered to return to their communes. Through this system, China has been able to avoid the large numbers of unemployed peasants who flocked to cities such as Cairo and Calcutta.

RESOURCES

Barnett, Tony and Piers Blakie. <u>AIDS in Africa: Its Present and Future Impact</u>. NY: Guilford Press, 1992.

Economist. <u>Book of Vital World Statistics</u>. An excellent resource, updated each year, with statistics ranging from GDP to deforestation.

Greer, Charles E. <u>China Facts and Figures Annual</u>. Gulf Breeze, FL: Academic International Press, 1992.

Kidron, Michael and Ronald Segal. <u>New State of the World Atlas</u>. NY: Simon & Schuster. An all new edition will be out in late March of 1995. Also available from CTIR Publications.

Liu, William T. <u>China Statistical Abstract 1988</u>. NY: Praeger, 1989.

Otero, George and Gary Smith. <u>Teaching about Food and Hunger</u>. Denver: CTIR Publications, University of Denver, 1989. A series of teaching activities that deal with aspects of food and hunger in our global society.

Sivard, Ruth. <u>World Military and Social Expenditures</u>. Washington, D.C.: World Priorities, Inc. An annual report about global interconnections between military and social priorities, poor and rich countries, world conflicts, and intervention by foreign powers. Teacher's manual available upon request.

World Bank. <u>Development Data Book.</u> Washington, D.C.: World Bank, 1991, Useful student resource.

Additional Resources

Office of Global Education, National Council of Churches, has a number of videos that are available, usually at little or no cost, for rental. Contact them at 219/264-3102; PO Box 968, 28606 Phillips Street, Elkhart, IN 46515.

<u>Forbes</u>, a weekly periodical that contains economic information for companies around the world. During the third week of July they always update the list of 100 largest MNCs.

<u>Fortune</u>, a periodical similar to the above that lists the 500 largest industrial companies in the world.

"Earth Shapes." Distorted world projections that can be used in a variety of creative ways in the classroom. Available from Creative Publications, 1300 Villa Street, Montview, CA 94041; 415/988-1000.

<u>Standard Dictionary of Advertisers</u>. National Register Publishing Company, 5201 Old Orchard, Skokie, IL 6077. Identifies the parent company of every advertised food produced in the United States.

<u>Finance and Development</u>, published by the International Monetary Fund and the World Bank Quarterly.

Amnesty International is an excellent organization who continue to work in the area of human rights. There are many local offices around the world.

SPICE at Stanford University has a variety of teaching activity books on many subjects including Europe. SPICE, Littlefield Center, Room 14C, Stanford, CA 94305-5013; 415/723-1114.

Printed in the United States
79526LV00006B/11